ECONOMIC DEVELOPMENT: THE CHALLENGE OF THE 1980s

The Council of State Planning Agencies is a membership organization comprised of the planning and policy staff of the nation's governors. Through its Washington office, the Council provides assistance to individual states on a wide spectrum of policy matters. The Council also performs policy and technical research on both state and national issues. The Council was formed in 1966; it became affiliated with The National Governors' Association in 1975.

In addition to *Studies in State Development Policy,* the Council publishes:

■ *CSPA Working Papers.* Current volumes address: environmental protection and economic development; commercial bank financing for small business enterprise; venture capital and urban development; the impact of regional shopping malls; the operation of minority capital markets; and the public service costs of alternative development patterns. A full list of current volumes is available on request.
■ *State Planning Issues.* A journal concerning the problems and practice of planning in the states. Published twice yearly.
■ *The State Planning Series.* Sixteen short papers dealing with financial management, citizen participation, econometrics, urban and rural development, policy development techniques, multi-state organizations, federal-state partnerships, and other issues of concern to state officials.

To order *Studies in State Development Policy* see page 71.

The Council of State Planning Agencies
Hall of the States
444 North Capitol Street
Washington, D.C. 20001
(202) 624-5386

Robert N. Wise
Director

Michael Barker
Associate Director for
Community and Economic Development

ECONOMIC DEVELOPMENT: THE CHALLENGE OF THE 1980s

NEAL R. PEIRCE
JERRY HAGSTROM
CAROL STEINBACH

COVER: "Map 1963," by Jasper Johns. Collection Albert Saalsfield. Grateful acknowledgement is made to Mr. Johns for allowing the reproduction of his work.

Partial funding support for this volume was received from the Office of Economic Research, Economic Development Administration, the U.S. Department of Commerce. The views and findings it contains are the author's, and do not necessarily represent those of the Economic Development Administration or the members or staff of The Council of State Planning Agencies. Reproduction of any part of this volume is permitted for any purpose of the United States Government.

Library of Congress Catalog Number: 79-54265

ISBN: 0-934842-00-0

Printed in the United States of America. First printing - 1979.

Format conceptualization and series coordination: Katherine Kinsella
Design: Kathy Jungjohann
Typesetting and Layout: Teri Grimwood
Printing and binding services: George Banta Co.

TABLE OF CONTENTS

EXECUTIVE SUMMARY *1*

INTRODUCTION *7*

1   "STATE OF THE ART" *11*

2   "SMOKESTACK CHASING" *16*

3   TAX INCENTIVES *22*

4   STATE PLANNING AND COORDINATION *27*

5   PEOPLE AND PLACES WITH SPECIAL NEEDS *30*

6   ENCOURAGING SMALL BUSINESS *37*

7   MANPOWER TRAINING *44*

8   ECONOMIC ANALYSIS *51*

9   THE INTERNATIONAL ANGLE *58*

APPENDIX A *65*

APPENDIX B *69*

APPENDICES

APPENDIX A

Table 1
Annual Rate of Employment Change for States by
Growth Rate of State *65*

Table 2
Percent Distribution of New Jobs Created in Each Region
Between 1974 and 1976 by Age of Establishment *66*

Table 3
Percentage of Total Jobs Generated by Size and Status
for Regions and the U.S. Between 1960 and 1976 .... *67*

Table 4
Status of Firms vs. Employment Gains by Region,
1969-72, 1972-74, 1974-76 .... *68*

APPENDIX B

Table 5
Regions Ranked by Number of Foreign Projects per Million Persons;
Number of Plants, 1975; Number of Acquisitions and
Constructions, 1975-1977, Third Quarter; and Number of
Constructions, 1975-1977, Third Quarter *69*

Table 6
States Ranked by Number of Foreign Projects per Million
Persons; Number of Plants, 1975; Number of Acquisitions and
Constructions, 1975-1977, Third Quarter; and Number of
Constructions, 1975-1977, Third Quarter *70*

EXECUTIVE SUMMARY

Economic development is essential to and inseparable from the successful governance of states. State economic development efforts should have no less a goal than creating a greater breadth of opportunity for all of a state's people, privileged and underprivileged alike. They are appropriate in every state, whether growing or declining, North, West or "Sunbelt." Such efforts should be related to and coordinated with virtually every other type of state activity and particularly efforts in education, manpower use, land use, taxation, health, rural development, the environment and future of cities.

The requisite coordination and focus of economic development activities is not possible without the personal interest and commitment of the governor. The chief executive alone has the authority to formulate an overall state strategy and oblige individual departments, traditionally busy with their own agendas and responding to their particular constituencies, to take heed of and reorient their activities around the state's basic economic growth strategy.

States have been involved in some form of economic development (special inducements to certain types of economic activity, for instance) since the earliest days of the Republic. But no accepted "textbook" of economic development exists; the literature is sparse. In practice, there may be only a thin line between legitimate state encouragement of economic activity and unconscionable raids on the public treasury for such purposes. Today's challenge is to make the state an active entrepreneur—or helper of entrepreneurs—in a fair and politically acceptable way.

State economic development efforts ought to de-emphasize assistance to large firms which are usually able to function effectively without state involvement beyond a reasonably fair tax and regulatory system. The alternative is to turn state activities toward retention of existing businesses of all sizes, promotion of growth of industries already in a state, a manpower system that legitimately connects applicants with jobs, and finally the nurturing of brand new industries.

State power to influence economic development is far greater than most governors or legislators realize. States have broad fiscal/tax, regulatory and expenditure policies which, when used in a concerted, well-planned manner, can have immense impact on the welfare of a state's citizens and communities.

State economic development agencies differ vastly in their size, *1*

scope and budgets. Some have large advertising budgets, others min-
iscule; some roll out red-carpet jet treatment for visiting industrialists,
others have far more modest programs; some are deeply involved in
technical assistance, others not. Many help businesses jump over
regulatory barriers; some states now have "one stop" shopping for
regulatory permits.

But instead of trying to focus the state's broad fiscal, regulatory and
expenditure policies in a way that effectively promotes economic
development for all the state's residents, many state development
agencies have let themselves become dangerously preoccupied with
"smokestack chasing"—the indiscriminate hunt for out-of-state
industries. Such a focus is ill-advised because research shows only a
tiny fraction of employment gains are due to instate moves, while an
overwhelming majority of job gains come from birth and expansion
of independent corporations, and not from branch plants, headquarters or relocation of multi-plant operations. Plants lured from
another state or region cost jobs in the areas they leave, nationally
a zero-sum game of economics far less attractive than the "win-win"
strategy of generating fresh economic activity. Often firms moving
into an area have such specialized labor requirements that the local
labor force gets few jobs, and those the more menial ones. New
plant locations place heavy burdens on local infrastructures and tax
bases. If cheap labor is the objective, the firm may stop only for a few
years before leaving for even lower labor costs in Mexico, Taiwan or
South Korea. Finally, localities or states may make so many concessions (tax abatements and the like) that they experience a very
small net "profit"—if any at all—from the industry they've captured.

States have become so busy offering tax incentives to firms that the
process may have become clearly counterproductive. Indeed, Michigan Governor William Milliken says just that: "We're just outbidding
each other. We're vying for the same companies. Each [state] is trying
to put in more incentives, more tax abatement programs and the like.
There has to be some point of marginal utility . . . when it will become
counterproductive within the country." In some states, tax abatement
programs have led to serious erosion of the tax base, a policy which
can lead to inadequate schools and services—some of the most
important drawing cards for industry in the first place. No state
seems to have broken this vicious cycle. State economic development
officials tend to praise special tax breaks; independent economists
and others overwhelmingly disparage them.

"State plans" are now produced by most states, but they vary
immensely in scope and quality. Some provide only the broadest
guidelines for economic development activities; others may be quite
2 specific about what kind of economic development (industrial,

agricultural, commercial, etc.) should take place and where. Too frequently, however, these plans are drawn in relative isolation from what is actually happening in the private marketplace. If plans are to point the way for future policy, the planning function must become more closely aligned with other functions of government under the coordination of the governor.

A realistic, coordinated state plan could bring together the dozens of state-funded programs that affect economic development to one degree or another. The result would be coordination among agencies that now frequently work at crosspurposes and greater efficiency in the expenditure of state funds. A state plan could provide the framework under which a range of state agencies—departments of community affairs, manpower services, business development, energy, transportation, agriculture, human services, education, welfare—could work together toward economic development goals they could not achieve alone.

Every state has areas that cry out for special attention—poor rural areas, declining cities, or mining boom towns with grave problems controlling growth. But most state officials do not consider it within their power to direct economic growth to needy areas of the state or restrict it in "superheated" economies. It would seem apparent, however, that the welfare of citizens and communities, not the convenience of industry, is the appropriate priority of a publicly-funded agency. State governments—by targeting their own expenditures and, where possible, the funds they receive from the federal government—could play a much greater role in encouraging development in those areas that need it most. Several states have pioneered in this area, most notably Massachusetts, which targeted its public investments to city and town centers, rather than providing money for sewers and roads in underdeveloped areas.

But targeting to the people and places most in need of economic assistance will not just "happen." It requires competent department heads and the support of a governor who (1) insists on the implementation of such policies and (2) is willing to exert the time and effort to achieve coordination of the disparate activities of the bureaucracies in our still-slumbering giants, America's state governments.

A field with tremendous potential for state economic development efforts is small business. Compared with other state economic development programs, current support for small business amounts to little more than lip service. There is no question that it is difficult to work individually with a great many small businesses, scattered around the state. Improving the climate for smaller enterprises, however, could have important implications for job creation and the state's *3*

The challenge today is to make the state an active entrepreneur—or helper of entrepreneurs—in a fair and politically acceptable manner.

---

pattern of business ownership. It is significant that the Northeastern and Midwestern regions of the country have not only the lowest rate of new enterprise development, but also the slowest rate of employment growth. Small business is jeopardized today by increasing government regulation, tax laws that encourage large companies to acquire small ones, and the increasing amount of capital controlled by conservatively-invested pension funds. Innovative programs of assistance to small business are in their infancy, but Connecticut and Massachusetts have established institutions to provide both capital and management assistance to small firms. Other avenues of assistance include "ombudsmen" to help small operators wade through state regulation and domestic and foreign marketing aid to small manufacturers and agricultural producers.

Every state has a job training program, but only a few appear to be making a significant impact on economic development in the state. Too often, these programs suffer from serious fragmentation, poor information resources and research capability, a lack of relevance to the realities of the labor market, and ineffective coordination between job training and job placement. Obviously, improving job training efforts alone will not solve all of a state's labor market problems. The single most effective employment strategy is a strong economy. But job training programs can play an important role in supporting a state's overall economic development effort. Job training can be one more element of public expenditure policy that is targetted to small businesses, distressed areas, minority residents, or other state economic development priorities.

Good, rigorous research on state economic issues is rare. The result is that neither politicians nor state economic development officers have much confidence in their understanding of the state's economy. Most end up producing unimaginative development strategies or none at all. Planners and economists have ignored state issues in favor of national economic policy or urban affairs, and state legislatures have rarely seen the need to pay for research. When research has been conducted, it has rarely asked the basic questions that might suggest new directions in development policy or inquired whether new industry actually creates jobs for current residents of the state.

Several states have begun limited economic research programs. The key to running an economic analysis unit on a limited budget,

California chief business economist Andrew Safir said, is to make use of existing information produced by banks and other institutions in the state and to place a priority on research which can be widely used. A major question facing state economic development officers is the adoption of econometric modeling to predict the future economy of the state and devise means to affect it. The models are expensive to develop and their accuracy has been questioned by many experts. The private sector and the federal government are increasingly relying on models, however, and the states may need to adopt them to have access to an equal volume and quality of information.

Foreign investment in the United States has expanded dramatically in the 1970s—doubling in the past five years alone,—uncovering rich new opportunities for state economic development departments.

In their rush to tap the foreign gold mine, states have established overseas offices and embarked on recruitment missions, undertaken expensive port expansions, put together large incentive packages for foreign firms, spent millions to advertise in overseas publications, and begun to publish their own world trade directories and newsletters.

It seems likely, however, that some states are overemphasizing the promotional aspects of foreign recruitment and neglecting the creative analysis that can reveal what kinds of foreign investment are most needed in the state.

Recruitment missions and overseas offices do have important "diplomatic" and "public relations" value, but excessive state spending on these functions may be foolish. What is likely more important is the "personal touch": a warm reception for visiting industrialists, a well-prepared, cordial development staff which understands federal and state laws that may confuse overseas investors, and a personal greeting from the governor.

One area where state governments can play an extremely useful role, particularly for small and medium-sized firms, is in the dissemination of information on exporting and trade. An increasing number of these firms wish to expand their markets abroad, but do not understand the foreign marketplace. State-sponsored exporting seminars, guides, inventories of trade leads, trade shows and the like can help provide the necessary expertise.

INTRODUCTION

Economic development is not an "optional" activity for state governments.

By action or inaction, interest or disinterest, state governments make daily decisions which have profound effects on the economic future of their states.

No governor, no state administration can disregard that the states' actions, in every field from taxation to encouragement of specific types of business activity, can play a major role in the lives of the states' citizens, rich or poor.

Nor is the problem confined to any region. The Northeast and Midwest, for instance, must look for fresh growth potentials to offset the declines inherent in a mature economy. A state like California, with increasing wage levels and heavy regulation, needs to reassure private business of its care and solicitude. The Mountain West must cope with high-pressure energy-based development problems. The South must learn to influence growth in a way that avoids the errors of the North and leverages economic growth to relieve high levels of poverty and serious minority unemployment.

Moreover, all states must recognize that a sound economy translates into a sound tax base, which in turn is the prerequisite for effective governance, no matter what one's political or philosophic predilections.

Indeed, economic development is of such central importance that it cannot be viewed as "one" of "many" problems a governor faces. To make any discernible difference, economic development must relate intimately to what a state government is seeking to do in better education, manpower use, transportation, land use, health, rural development, the environment and future of cities. This means there is no substitute for the continuous deep involvement of the governor. Regardless of the precise organizational structure of a state's economic development effort, the governor must personally lead as chief executive of state government in pulling together all relevant efforts to expand economic opportunity.

Despite its central importance, economic development has long been a source of profound confusion in state capitals. No accepted "textbook" of its administration exists; the literature is sparse. Special interests, for example, assiduously support special tax abatements and the like. Their position may or may not be correct;

the fact is that virtually no articulated criticisms of such policies are accessible to political leaders.

This is not to say that state involvement in economic activity, some of it highly controversial, has not existed throughout our history. Even before the Revolutionary War, the colonies introduced an extensive system of bounties, tax incentives and even legal monopolies to foster the production of goods. Carried on in the early decades of the young Republic, state subsidies ranged from foodstuffs to beer to home utensils, all on the assumption some special need was required to get young enterprises off the ground. On a broader canvas, state development of ports, of turnpikes, of canals and railroads all played an integral role in the economic expansion of these United States.

The dilemma, the quandary, is that at each step of our national development, the methods that appeared to some to be reasonable state measures to encourage commerce and manufacturing could be (and ofter were) interpreted by others as unconscionable raids on the public treasury for the benefit of a few, or as public sustenance of monopoly, or both.

The challenge today is to make the state an active entrepreneur—or helper of entrepreneurs—in a fair and politically acceptable manner. Large economic enterprises, for the most part, are able to function effectively without state involvement beyond a reasonably fair tax and regulatory system.

The alternative will be to turn state economic activities to all-too-often neglected fields: retention of existing economic enterprises of all sizes, promotion of the growth of industries already in a state, a manpower system that effectively connects applicants with jobs, and finally the nurturing of brand new economic enterprises—those new corporations or partnerships which have the greatest potential, on a cumulative basis, to generate new economic growth and jobs.

"Smokestack chasing" often results in a zero-sum game of economic development, each state clawing for jobs at the expense of another. All states could establish a win-win strategy, however, by adopting activist policies which assist expanding in-state firms and aid, in every area from venture capital to technical expertise, the incubation of new enterprises appropriate to local economic strengths and realities.

Is state government capable of such a challenge? Across the nation, state governments have advanced dramatically in recent decades in executive organization, professional competence, legislative "representativeness," and broad-based tax systems. Without adding any further to the size of government, states may now be asked: How can you use that increased potential for the most important job of all, the well-being of your citizens?

8   Specifically, states should abandon the habit of suggesting that

because of the weight of the federal tax system, the hundreds of federal grant-in-aid programs, federal fiscal, regulatory and monetary policies, they are powerless to effect their own destinies. The fact is that the states retain the basic sovereignty—the capacity to act across broad fronts, unencumbered by limited delegations of authority—which was granted them under the federal system. Often they simply lack the political will to act aggressively.

Instead of state defeatism, the time may be more appropriate for the federal government to wonder whether some national programs and goals have not overreached attainable objectives, and particularly whether the time has not come to consider far more seriously the capacity of states to act decisively and efficiently, sensitive to local needs and conditions, to improve the economy within their own borders.

States cannot force the federal government to change its attitudes. But by their own actions in a field as central as economic development, they can demonstrate their own relevance, their power, and most importantly their ability to improve the quality of life available to citizens of all economic backgrounds.

1

"STATE OF THE ART"

State power to influence economic development is far greater than most governors or legislators realize. States, for example, administer the bulk of federal funds for roads, sewers, parks and other public facilities, and provide more direct financial aid to their localities than the federal government. Cities, counties and towns are constitutionally their creations; states can alter their boundaries, shift powers, make annexation easy or virtually impossible, and determine which localities can tax and for what purpose. They can establish and fund special agencies to finance new jobs and business development, training programs and housing. In conservation, the environment, land use, the administration of justice, transportation, education, health and economic development, state powers are immense.

In general, state activities affecting economic development fall into three categories: fiscal/tax policy, regulatory policy and expenditure policy.

State fiscal policies may be said to include all state tax laws—preeminently personal income and sales taxes, local taxes (property, sales and others) which the state authorizes, and special exemptions or abatements in taxes, whether levied by the state or its localities. As noted in a subsequent chapter, the level of business taxes and the number of tax abatements for industry have far less of an impact on business investment decisions than is often assumed.

Taken more broadly, however, fiscal policies can have a positive impact on economic development. Authorizing localities to raise non-property tax revenues—such as payroll or commuter taxes—enhancing local borrowing capacity, financing more services at the state level, tax base sharing, and relaxing municipal annexation laws are fiscal actions that can greatly benefit needy areas.

State regulatory policies refer to the host of laws regulating land use and the environment, water and sewage, the chartering of banks, the licensing of restaurants, the issuance of building permits and numerous other actions which strongly influence who can engage in certain economic ventures and under what circumstances.

Taken on their own, state regulations do not make for a very effective economic development strategy. They are frequently too reactive, too susceptible to influence by special interests, generally disliked by business and, if too strict, a deterrent to economic growth. When combined with other fiscal and expenditure actions, state *11* regulatory policy can play a useful role in promoting economic activity. But ironically, it is often the streamlining of permit procedures and requirements which has the greatest positive impact on economic growth.

The third type of state policy, expenditure policy, can be a far more powerful tool in economic development than either of the other two. How much money a state spends, what it spends it on and where can a be a potent force in the financial health of residents and communities throughout the state. "The immediate impact of state expenditure is the jobs and incomes directly created, along with the multiplier effect of this increase in economic activity," said Belden Daniels of Harvard University. "When a state hospital, college or office complex is constructed, it confers benefits on the area surrounding its site. Although those employed by state spending account for only 4 percent of employment nationwide, the most important influence of the state budget on economic development comes through the goods and services provided by expenditures, many of which, of course, touch the operation of private firms."

The success of a state's economic development program depends enormously on the willingness and ability of the chief executive to use the tax, regulatory and expenditure tools of state government in a concerted fashion. It also requires careful planning, well-thought out strategies developed in cooperation with local officials and the legislature.

Every state has an agency or group of agencies handling economic development, but their breadth and scope vary widely. In some states, the agency's overall budget is but a few hundred thousand dollars, while others spend in excess of that for advertising alone. Some states limit their activities to small scale promotional efforts or minor technical assistance to localities seeking economic growth. For others economic development is a multi-million dollar activity, involving elaborate advertising campaigns and foreign recruitment missions, red carpet treatment for visiting industrialists (including site tours in the state helicopter), detailed economic analysis and special programs to train local officials in the art of economic development.

Despite all this activity, few states are fashioning fiscal, regulatory and expenditures policies in a way that most effectively promotes economic development.

A number of state officials feel that economic development is the type of activity that gains attention and support when conditions are bad and tends to be de-emphasized when conditions are good. In 1966 in Florida, for example, unemployment was low and the economy strong. The following year the economic development staff was cut from 55 to eight, the budget sliced from $3.5 million to $50.000. "The legislature wanted us to depend only on tourists," says Bureau of Trade Development Director Dick Brock. But with the Arab boycott and gas shortages, tourism declined and unemployment rose above the national average for the first time in Florida's history. "It scared the hell out of everybody," says Brock. The result: the legislature in 1975 tripled the economic development budget and staff.

"A lot of states have never really gotten serious about their economic development program," one state economic development director said. "Every three or four years the entire agency turns over. The governor makes a political appointment who might not know the first thing about site selection. You wipe the slate clean and lose all your contacts. It's counterproductive."

A number of state economic development activities—particularly tax incentives—appear to have as their underlying rationale the desire to establish credibility with the business community and to demonstrate a state's seriousness in wanting industrial development. "If you ask the average businessman about state government, he would say he wishes it would go away," said Norton Birman, Michigan's Director of Economic Expansion. "Credibility is something we constantly have to establish."

To this end, nearly every state spends funds promoting itself as an advantageous site for business. Advertising budgets in some, like Alaska ($2,000 in 1977) and Wyoming ($8,000 in 1977) are modest, but at least 10 states spent more than $250,000 on advertising campaigns in 1977, according to the National Association of State Development Agencies. Seven million dollars was spent in magazine advertising alone in 1977, and the number of ads jumped by 40 percent in the first quarter of 1978.

Most states have a program to help prospective industries find suitable sites for their plants, and some are quite extensive. In one state, for example, a representative of the state economic development office uses the state jet to shepherd visiting industrialists to suitable site locations, which are exacted by feeding the firm's site requirements into a state computer. Planning and research specialists prepare marketing data on the prospective firm to show its opportunities in the state and surrounding markets. The state geologist researches mineral resources and tests possible sites for their ability to support the industry, while a community data sheet, updated annually, lists all available buildings for the industry. Manpower specialists describe what labor is available, with promises made to train the industry's workforce at no expense, and environmental consultants explain regulatory requirements.

State economic development offices frequently try to help business wend its way through the state regulatory structure. California last 13 year re-established its economic development office because it found it was losing industries due to red tape and bureaucratic bungling, creating a perception that the state was inhospitable to business.

Several states—California, Washington, Oregon, Minnesota and others—are trying to simplify the bureaucracy for business by establishing "one-stop shops" for regulatory permits. Other states are considering similar actions.

Officials interviewed said they would not try to skirt a state regulation or negotiate to have one waived for a specific industry. But many do act as a business advocate, lobbying the legislature for changes in a state's tax code or a relaxation of environmental standards, or arranging meetings and consultations between the regulators and the regulated. "We are not the advocate for violating the law," says Florida's Dick Brock, "but for removing bureaucratic roadblocks."

Providing technical assistance to localities is another activity of most state economic development offices, although here, too, the scope varies widely. A few states help their communities develop and pursue broad economic goals. Massachusetts, for example, used an elaborate procedure for surveying its localities to determine their development priorities and turned the results into the nation's most comprehensive state growth strategy. In Florida, the Bureau of Economic Analysis produces a detailed profile of its 67 counties, recommending specific economic goals for each. These are modified after consultation with local officials. "We do not impose on them Tallahassee ideas," says Brock. "If they want an apparel plant, we don't say you have to have electronics. We feel they're the ones who should establish their goals, and we'll do everything to help." The process, in short, becomes one of negotiation between the state and its localities. The state can use its powers of persuasion, but actual state efforts to force an economic strategy on a recalcitrant locality would probably prove counterproductive. The process of give and take is even more complicated in the state's negotiations with large cities, which have their own economic development departments and strong financial institutions with development strategies of their own.

In most states, "help" means preparing small towns to handle industrial prospects. Many, like Nebraska, publish comprehensive manuals for town officials outlining strategies for attracting and impressing visiting industrialists. Michigan is among the states which help organize and fund community associations of local officials and business and labor representatives to promote economic development.

"Prospects are impressed with community leaders that know what they're talking about and have a style of promotion at the local level
which is efficient, attractive and knowledgeable," says Robert Leak,

Taken on their own, state regulations do not make for a very effective economic development strategy. They are frequently too reactive, too susceptible to influence by special interests . . .

---

director of South Carolina's Development Board, which runs a "Great Towns" program to prepare localities "for the day when a live prospect may walk in the door. We go in first and clean up the town and make it look good physically," says Leak. "Then we organize the local leaders into a sales team and we train them on what they need to know about their town and how to present it. We give them a notebook of questions most frequently asked by prospects, require them to get property under control for industrial sites and to work out in advance water and sewage activities. We're a jack-of-all-trades to help them prepare."

While promotional activities are not without their place in state economic development programs, too often, it appears, they are used as a substitute for well-coordinated fiscal, regulatory and expenditure strategies. In their enthusiasm to attract industry, state officials may not always have their eye on the right ball—a question treated in the following chapter.

2

"SMOKESTACK CHASING"

"Another war is going on between the states these days but this one doesn't mean bloodshed—only hard feelings.

"The spoils—millions of dollars in business and thousands of jobs.

"The battleground can be anywhere—a state's governor's office, a corporate board room, a foreign city. The participants are the states themselves as they muscle one another in attempts to entice an industry to pull up stakes and move all or part of its operations elsewhere."

With those words, United Press International reported September 3, 1978 on the fierce competition between the states for industrial locations—the popular sport known as "smokestack chasing."

No one can argue that there can be positive benefits for a state in capturing a business which exists elsewhere, or which might choose another location:

■ Industries do create jobs, with well-advertised spin-off effects in subsidiary employment and jobs created for suppliers, including small enterprises. The effect, particularly on small cities, can be great.

■ However well the citizens of a state may manufacture goods and provide services for each others' needs, they need wealth to "import" goods from other states. New industries add to that source of wealth.

■ It is often worthwhile for a state to seek to attract industries whose presence would create markets for new firms or those already located within the state. This creates, in short, an industrial market for other firms—a process of "import substitution."

Aware of these and other political benefits, many states invest an immense amount of time, money and energy in industrial recruiting. In many states, this activity appears to overshadow all other economic development efforts.

A strong argument, however, can be made that such efforts involve excessive costs, lead to abuses, and most serious of all, simply miss the mark of where the real potential lies for increased employment in the United States today.

Pioneering research by David L. Birch of the Massachusetts Institute of Technology, based on analysis of Dun and Bradstreet data tracing the behavior of 6.5 business establishments (about 80 percent of all jobs in the United States), first for 1969-72 and subsequently 1974-76, produced the following results:

■ Virtually no firms migrate these days from one area to another in the sense of hiring a moving van and relocating their operations. Thus, the activity known as "smokestack chasing"'—seeking firms from another state or region—largely misses the point. Only 0.5 percent of the new jobs in any state or region over a three-year period were found to result from the inter-state migration of firms. The average net shift (what a state might gain over what it might lose in a given three-year period due to firm migrations between states) was only 0.1 percent.

■ Firm deaths and contractions cause an 8 percent job loss at a uniform rate across the country. The difference between "growing" and "declining" areas is due almost entirely to the rate at which lost jobs are replaced by new firms and the expansion of existing ones. Southern and Western states have done better than those in the Northeast and Midwest, because they have a higher birth rate of new companies.

■ The overwhelming majority of new jobs come from the birth and expansion of young, small and independent corporations, not from branch plants, headquarters or the relocation of multiplant operations, although branch plants are relatively more important in the South.

■ Small firms are the country's biggest job generators. Two-thirds of all new jobs are in companies employing fewer than 20 people. Medium-sized and large firms generate relatively few new jobs. Studies of the top 1,000 firms on the *Fortune* listing show they added just 75,000 new jobs in the 1970-76 period, years in which the overall economy added 6.2 million jobs, or 82 times as many.

Notes Birch: "Development policies aimed at attracting new firms address a very small aspect of employment change, while policies aimed at assisting firms already in the state or firms wanting to get started here, hit at the heart of the matter."

Even between rural and metropolitan areas, Birch found firm migration plays a minor role in overall employment shifts. Nor does it seem likely that pirating firms from one region of the country to another ("Frostbelt" to "Sunbelt," for instance) is as significant in the nation's development as it may have been in the late 1960s and early 1970s. The increased birth rate of firms in the Sunbelt (both South and West) appears to be the more significant factor, according to the Birch studies. (In the 1970-72 period, for instance, births of new firms increased employment 4.6 percent in the Northeast and 4.9 percent in *17*

The overwhelming majority of new jobs come from the birth and expansion of young, small and independent corporations, not from branch plants, headquarters or the relocation of multiplant operations . . .

---

the Midwest, but 7.6 percent in the South and 7.3 percent in the West.) Thus to focus on runaway plants would appear to be a poor state strategy. (See Appendix A.)

Findings complementary to Birch's emerged from a study by Roger W. Schmenner of Harvard Business School (*The Manufacturing Location Decision: Evidence from Cincinnati and New England,* March 1978). Based on 40 interviews with company executives and public officials, over 1,000 completed surveys of manufacturing plants and 120 completed surveys of large corporations, Schmenner found that "the geographic pattern of employment change in urban areas is concentrated not with the largest employers in the area but with many small companies which are growing and in need of space, just getting started, or on the verge of failure." The facts of industrial location, Schmenner suggested, "argue for a policy of 'tending your own garden' " in three principal areas: (1) facilitating on-site expansion of companies already residing in the city or area; (2) helping small, growing plants, many of them recent incorporations, find new or additional space; and (3) promoting the city or area's advantages as an initial location for new incorporations and new branch plants.

While many governors and state economic development officials continue to stress the potential of recruitment of large out-of-state firms, others have begun to show severe skepticism.

Said former Massachusetts Secretary of Economic Affairs Howard Smith: "It's a mistake to make the main thrust of a state's program the attraction of new industry from out of state . . . We're not interested in barnstorming around, running color ads in *Fortune* about how great Massachusetts is. Sending governors and others on fishing expeditions is for show—it's not very real and not very cost effective."

In the UPI survey, the "contact making" policies of certain states were given significant mention. The Texas Industrial Commission boasted having recruited 13 firms in June 1978 alone.

But Jack Dressen, Director of Oklahoma's Industrial Development Corporation, said his state prefers to get companies to expand in Oklahoma rather than relocate to the state. Pam Knode of Alaska's Department of Commerce and Economic Development said "the primary goal right now is . . . not so much in trying to get companies to move here but to develop entirely new industries." An official of the

Maryland Department of Economic and Community Development said 70 to 80 percent of that state's new jobs come from expansion of existing plants.

Even when new plants are successfully recruited from outside, their blessings are not unmixed. A newly-relocated plant, for instance, may have specialized labor requirements which oblige it to bring a significant portion of its workforce with it. The number of jobs for local residents may be few, menial, or both. "We should ask," says Colorado Treasurer Roy Romer, "if this new 1,000-job industry is going to bring in 900 from the outside? Or it is going to employ 900 from the county where it locates?" New residents drawn by plant relocations place a burden on local schools and basic infrastructure that all taxpayers may be forced to share. In states with severe limitations on local property taxes (such as California in the post-Proposition 13 era), added annual operating costs of required new residential sub-divisions (fire, police, schools, etc.) may exceed anticipated tax revenue, not to mention the capital cost of new infrastructure.

"New plants that are controlled by corporations headquartered elsewhere impose enormous infrastructure costs on a community," Bennett Harrison and Sandra Kanter note in an article in *Working Papers for a New Society*. "They import much of their labor (especially the 'good' jobs), and they often house their highest-paid workers outside the taxing jurisdiction where the plant is situated. Then—after all the effort expended to get them in the first place—they often move to some other place when local inducements run out."

This is not to say that millions of strong, permanent U.S. jobs are not in plants of corporations with distant headquarters. But the growing trend of large multinational firms to shift jobs to areas of lowest pay and unionization levels—currently Mexico, Taiwan and South Korea—raises questions about the desirability of capturing firms unless they make a substantial capital investment and show a clear intent to remain in the new area for many years to come.

Smokestack chasing is often part and parcel of the excessive state tax incentives—what the *Wall Street Journal* has described as the "candy store of incentive programs"—reviewed in the next chapter. State industrial recruitment ads often stress low levels of state taxation in comparison to other states, or lower wages, or both. The low wage inducement traditional in Southern smokestack chasing, historian C. Vann Woodward has noted, led to "juleps for the few and pellegra for the crew." But even Northeastern areas, presumably cooperating in recent years to preserve their economic status, now resort to appeals based on low wages. Philadephia, close to suffering New York, has continued to run advertisements in the New York press offering "the **19** most reasonable wages" for office workers on the East Coast.

The Texas Industrial Commission ran television ads in New York City in Winter 1975, during a heavy blizzard and a period of high New York unemployment, trying to induce employers to shift to Texas. Nor is there any sign of a cutback in Texas' approach. In Autumn 1978, TIC was preparing a set of television commercials to show in Cleveland the following February, when that Great Lakes city could be expected to be suffering under a mantle of ice and snow. The planned television spot showed a block of ice appearing on the screen, then a hand wielding an ice pick and beginning to chip away at it, and a bass voice delivering the message:

> "About this time of year, the deep freeze can really get to your company—the ice, the snow, production slowdowns, socked-in transportation. But you can change all that in Texas and get productivity 16 percent above the average. In Texas, you can forget about state income taxes, personal and corporate, live better at less cost with a new Texas plant location. Dial the Texas Industrial Commission. There's more to talk about than the weather."

Should that campaign succeed, *The Texas Observer* notes, "by February of 1980 Cleveland residents will be not only cold but also unemployed." Texas decided to withdraw the ad when Cleveland went into default, "so as not to kick a fellow when he's down," according to a TIC official—who did not preclude using it in a future year.

The Texas ad points up the unfortunate element of smokestack chasing—"robbing of Peter to pay Paul," the zero-sum game of national economic gain which it implies.

The proliferation of tax breaks and other special concessions could also encourage increasing numbers of industries to play one state against another, get handsome concessions from all, and simply "leapfrog" among states with the most attractive current offers.

Questionable concessions unquestionably seemed involved in the struggle among Pennsylvania, Ohio and other states to capture a Volkswagen plant that would hire approximately 5,000 workers. Pennsylvania finally won, but at a heavy price including state expenditure of $40 million to buy and refurbish an old Chrysler plant for VW and then lease it back to VW for 30 years, the first 20 years at a tiny 1.75 percent interest rate. The state promised to float $10 million in bonds for a special railway spur, another $15 million for highway construction, to tap the public employees' pension fund for a $6 million loan to VW, and to have local authorities forego 95 percent of VW's taxes for the first two years and 50 percent for the following three years. According to critic Ron Chernow, "When you strip away the

20 rhetoric from the VW deal, you are left with the fact that Pennsylvania

. . . the growing trend of large multinational firms to shift jobs to areas of lowest pay and unionization levels —currently Mexico, Taiwan and South Korea—raises questions about the desirability of capturing firms unless they make a substantial capital investment and show a clear intent to remain in the new area for many years to come.

---

has made a risky, substantial investment in a privately-owned foreign corporation." The *Wall Street Journal* noted that Pennsylvania had "bestowed its favors so generously on a single investor that it threatens to impose burdens on other taxpayers."

In 1977 competition between Ohio and Michigan for a $500 million, 6,000-job Ford plant, both states—according to totals compiled by the *Chicago Daily News*—were willing to forgive future taxes and make direct grants in excess of $84 million. Ohio (the eventual winner) estimated state and local government would receive a net gain of only $500,000 for the first few years of the plant's operation, *Illinois Issues* reported.

Questioning how far Illinois should go in the "frantic competition" among the states for industries, *Illinois Issues* also noted: "States that buy land for out-of-state companies or provide low-interest loans for industrial land acquisition may actually be harming their old industrial base. First, they are creating tremendous ill will among the plants that have remained in the state for years . . . . It may not be long before such indigenous companies are testing the waters in neighboring states. Secondly, those states that subsidize new industry are creating unfair competition for their domestic plants, just as if they were directly subsidizing these firms' competitors."

A final potential abuse lies in the temptation for economic development arms of state government to exaggerate or even falsify the totals of jobs they have brought to the state in order to justify their own existence. *New Jersey Magazine,* in a study of what the New Jersey Economic Development Authority claimed it had achieved in 1975 and 1976, found that only 9 of the 71 manufacturing firms the agency loaned funds to had created as many jobs as EDA claimed, and that the agency had overstated the number of jobs it was creating by more than twice the actual number. While 5,874 jobs were claimed, the magazine found only 2,234 were actually delivered.

3

TAX INCENTIVES

A Massachusetts labor leader suggests there ought to be some kind of "SALT agreement" among the states to reduce the immense costs of tax abatements used in the interstate battle for industry. The Governor of Michigan tells us: "I'm increasingly troubled by the competition among the states. We're just outbidding each other. We're vying for the same companies. Each one is trying to put in more incentives, more tax abatement programs and the like. There has to be some point of marginal utility . . . when it will become counterproductive within the country."

Yet even the same governor (William Milliken) believes that without a special tax incentive Michigan had available, some major industrial "captures," including the retention of a 5,000-worker Chrysler plant in Detroit, would not have taken place.

There is no easy answer to what states ought to do about the myriad of special tax incentives they now offer: outright exemptions on property taxes for certain classes of business buildings and real estate; exemptions of sales taxes for goods used in manufacture; exemptions of taxes on inventories; lower severance taxes on mineral extraction; lower corporate or personal income taxes; state guarantees of all or portions of the costs of plant manufacture; authorization for state loans to new businesses; investment tax credits for property, buildings and equipment; general or revenue industrial bonds; even a "hidden" form of tax incentive in such devices as lower unemployment compensation fund payments.*

The state which fails to offer such inducements may feel the risk inordinate: that it is unlikely to gain industries that might otherwise choose it as a location. The state which offers too many of them finds its revenues seriously depleted, a policy which can lead to inadequate schools and public facilities—some of the most important drawing cards for industry in the first place.

Apparently no state has found a way to break this vicious cycle. State economic development officials tend to praise the special tax

---

*For details on the principal types of tax incentives offered to industries, see *Book of the States: 1978-79 edition,* pages 491 ff. These charts illustrate graphically how rapidly the number of special state tax incentives and other programs to aid industry have grown since the mid-1960s. The most liberal exemption of all is probably Puerto Rico's: that territory exempts manufacturers of goods first produced in Puerto Rico after 1946 from both property and income taxes for up to 25 years.

breaks; independent economists and other observers overwhelmingly disparage them.

"Policymakers should be skeptical of fiscal incentives as an economic development tool," according to a report by the Academy for Contemporary Problems, a research institution which operates under the direction of governors, state legislators, mayors and other governmental public interest groups. "Although existing research is far from conclusive, and a definitive test may never be carried out," the Academy reported, "the overwhelming consensus is that tax and fiscal concessions rarely have much effect on interstate or interregional choice of industrial location. Where adjacent states place sharply different tax burdens on industry, there may indeed be some noticeable locational effect."

To the left of the ideological spectrum, the conclusions are even more negative. In *Working Papers for a New Society,* Bennett Harrison and Sandra Kanter made the point in the strongest imaginable terms. "No economic policy has been more poorly argued and documented, yet so uniformly and warmly supported by special interest lobbyists," they wrote. "These business incentives do not produce new output or jobs. They do have real costs in the form of foregone tax revenues which have valuable alternative uses. It is also possible that some of these incentives raise the price that state governments and less privileged private investors have to pay for borrowing capital from the private sector."

Such analyses base their criticisms on evidence that the costs of land, transportation, energy, labor and construction are far more important than the cost of taxes to industry. "Variations in business taxes among the states are far less than the wide range in wages paid per $100 of profits," the Academy noted. "State tax differences per $100 of profit have a range of around $25, while wage differences per $100 of profit exceed $250." Tax incentives may make a difference in locational decisions within a metropolitan area, the Academy asserted, but the states' authorization for local tax breaks may also have negative side effects. Communities in the same state may end up competing with one another via tax concessions for new business. "From the standpoint of the state," the Academy noted, "such a competition is at best a zero-sum game."

Even theoreticians who helped devise revenue bond programs are critical of them. University of Wisconsin business professor Jon Udell helped create the revenue bond program in his state, but said afterward it would be better to let the basic economic determinants prevail. "In the aggregate, it's economically inefficient," Udell said. "With each business located in the best possible location, you have the lowest cost and the greatest productivity in the industry." **23**

Although business lobbyists have given strong support to tax incentives over the years, there is less than unanimous support for the idea even from private firms. Several questionnaire studies have shown that businessmen, when asked directly, tend to give substantial weight to the role of taxes in industrial location decisions. But when asked to list the considerations in location in order of importance, taxes drop to fifth place after labor costs, market, availability of labor, and industrial climate.

More recently, some business executives have openly said that incentives are no substitute for a sound tax system. "The free ride of a two or five-year tax moratorium while capital costs are recovered is not the solution," said Lewis Lehr, president of U.S. operations for the 3M Company. "Industry in some of the states which used this lure is discovering that, sooner or later, somebody has to pay for state services."

Perhaps the strongest indictment of all comes from John Thodis, executive director of the Michigan Manufacturers' Association. Incentives, Thodis said, are the states' equivalent of the salt lick that deer hunters put out in a clearing while they wait in the woods ready to shoot. A smart businessman, Thodis concluded, will not be bamboozled by short-term attractions and long-term costs.

Even critics of tax incentives acknowledge, however, that the incentives do perform a valuable psychological function in assuring business that the state has an interest in economic development. At the very least, state officials can point to the incentives when inquiring industrialists ask what the state does for business. "Everyone wants to be wanted," as one state economic development official said.

It can be argued, however, that both business and the citizenry would be better served by an efficient state government taxing at a fair rate and offering a high quality of services.

Instead of passing additional tax gimmicks, governors and legislators could serve business quite effectively by concentrating on improving state services and re-examining the basic tax structure for specific items which may be curbing business development.

As the Academy of Contemporary Problems concluded, other means of encouraging growth and development are readily at hand— "cutting down on red tape, providing adequately for public services essential to efficient business operation, assisting firms to find suitable sites, and offering a hospitable and attractive community environment."

Wisconsin may provide the best example of a state that has used a reputation for "good government" to overcome the disincentive of relatively high taxes. Due particularly to a high and quite progressive income tax, Wisconsin residents pay $138 in state and local taxes for each $1000 they earn, compared with the national average of $123 per $1000.* Overall, Wisconsin is the seventh highest tax state in the country. Manufacturing wages are also high, and the state is heavily unionized.

Yet business is expanding more rapidly in Wisconsin than in most other states in the generally high-tax Northeast-Midwest region. (Several Sunbelt states, of course, have more rapid rates of expansion.) Several reasons are given for Wisconsin's success. Wisconsin state government, by national standards, is quite efficient and as corruption-free as any state in the Union. A second explanation is that high productivity among Wisconsin workers is traditional. Finally, the state in 1973 enacted a tax cut eliminating the property tax on machinery and equipment—a step supported by both business and labor. (As noted earlier, Wisconsin has also passed a tax incentive program, but business analysts believe it is much less significant than other state "reforms.")

Some Wisconsin state officials still find it difficult to judge the value of the tax cut, but an exodus of jobs out of the state did stop after it was passed. Until 1973, Wisconsin's tax on equipment and machinery was the second highest in the nation. According to Professor Udell, "The 1973 tax change made it possible for other inherent advantages in Wisconsin to become operative once again."

Despite the evidence that tax abatements are of limited value at best, there exists no strong political drive to discontinue them. Those states that do continue tax abatement programs might well protect themselves by targeting the grants, loans or tax credits exclusively to new projects, or by requiring recipients to adhere to certain goals. Chronic problems such as low per capita income levels and high unemployment may warrant granting abatement powers to some localities, but the state should insist the localities meet certain specific requirements, noted James Cullison, director of Florida's Bureau of Economic Analysis.

States might also adopt tax expenditure disclosure requirements which would make public the revenue losses resulting from abatements of all types. Such disclosure requirements, enacted in Wisconsin, California and Maryland, make it easier for the lawmaker

---

*Several high state officials interviewed believed very low or nonexistent state income taxes are major inducements to executives of industries considering locating in a state. Unquestionably, there are instances where this is true. The challenge to a state with a relatively high state income tax is to prove to the prospective firm that the state offers substantial service and "quality of life" benefits which make the extra tax investment a worthwhile one. Since the Advisory Commission on Intergovernmental Relations and most other tax authorities recommend an income tax as part of a state's tax "mix," the onus should be on the state to provide service and quality benefits to justify the income tax, rather than suggesting that income taxes be repealed or not approved on the chimerical chance that some out-of-state firm might be attracted.

Incentives . . . are the states' equivalent of the salt lick that deer hunters put out in a clearing while they wait in the woods ready to shoot. A smart businessman . . . will not be bamboozled by short-term attractions and long-term costs.

---

and the taxpayer to judge the cost of tax relief, to identify the number of beneficiaries and to determine if the original beneficiaries are still deserving of the tax subsidy.

The bottom line would seem to be that in an era of Proposition-13 like tax stringency at state and local levels, it is not only foolish but clearly against the public will to "give away the store" to lure industry which might locate in a state anyway. Even if some grand "SALT agreement" can never be reached among the states to reduce unnecessary tax inducements, the subject might be discussed more thoroughly and candidly at meetings of governors and other high state officials. And through a policy of generally reducing ineffective tax inducements, the states might conceivably realize the benefits of a "SALT agreement" without the agony (and probable frustrating defeat) of attempting line-by-line negotiation.

4
STATE PLANNING AND COORDINATION

In an "ideal" state government, development officials might be supplied with a comprehensive and usable state plan into which their own efforts would fit—just as departments responsible for education, transportation, energy, agriculture, health or other services would fit into the state plan.

In fact, "state plans" are now produced in all states of the Union. In some instances, the state itself has seen the need for such an activity; in many more, the availability of federal grants for such activities seems to be the activating factor. Under the Economic Development Administration's 302 program, for instance, all states are asked to draw up an economic development plan. The Department of Housing and Urban Development and other federal grant-giving agencies require still other plans.

The plans produced vary immensely in scope and quality. Some provide only the broadest guidelines for economic development activities; others may be quite specific, detailing where or how development activities (industrial, commercial, agricultural, etc.) can best take place. Out of the planners' office emerge plans which do not, as so many activities of economic development offices do, respond exclusively to business concerns. Their authors intend them to rest on some more expansive concept of the "public interest." But if drawn by professional planners in relative isolation from the mainstream of state decision-making, they all too often gather dust on shelves.

Some states have instituted ambitious programs to gauge the wishes of the people on the future path of the state—Alternatives for Washington, Goals for Georgia, and others. On occasion, the results of those conferences and accompanying surveys are fed into the state planning document. But as valuable as they should be in pointing the way for future policy, they are almost as likely as etherially produced plans by planners to be ignored if the state executive does not take concrete steps to see they are adhered to.

"Plans aren't worth a tinker's tooth unless you implement them," said Woody Brooks, Director of South Carolina's Division of Local Government. "And when one governor went out of office, there were two truckloads of plans taken from the basement where the water had come in and spoiled them. There's no telling how many millions went into them."

There is no way to prevent sharp switches in state policy (often quite needed) between governors. But a few state administrations have allowed their planners to become central players in the process of day-to-day state governance. In these instances, the planners have gradually acquired the requisite confidence of the governor to exercise some political power and oblige other state departments—including those concerned with economic development—to follow their lead. Frank Keefe, as state planning director under former Massachusetts Governor Michael Dukakis, headed the governor's development cabinet and became deeply involved with "bricks and mortar" physical redevelopment projects in many cities, as well as close work with industries. Keefe's planning office developed and administered a "state growth policy process" that went much further than most programs in building a true community consensus on the course of future development. As a result, even though Dukakis was defeated in 1978, there is still a strong measure of political support—among local officials, business leaders, and private citizens—for the growth policies adopted at the conclusion of the process. Bill Press, as Governor Edmund G. Brown's chief planner, acquired some of the same power as he put together the pieces of California's urban policy.

Such instances, unfortunately, are all too rare. "The split between planning in one place of government and implementation of programs in another results in some pretty shoddy communication," said the economic development officer of one state where agency coordination is considered better than most. "I'm not aware that the state has an economic plan. If it has, neither its opportunities nor its constraints have surfaced here."

These criticisms could be taken as simple anti-planning biases. But interviews with state development officials indicated a minimal number of cases where the planning function of state government was paid much heed—or even seemed to enter the commerce director's consciousness.

Some states appear to accept the EDA's "302" state planning grants simply for the sake of money, with no serious expectation of using the results. EDA provides little constructive feedback to states on the "302" planning products, and even when critical, renews states planning monies almost automatically. There also appears to be no consistent EDA effort to implement its other grant programs (Section 304, Title I, Title IX, Title II, etc.) in accordance with the state economic development plan the federal government has financed.

A realistic, coordinated state plan could bring together the dozens of state funded programs that affect a state's development. The result **28** would be coordination among agencies that now frequently work at cross-purposes and greater efficiency in the expenditure of state funds. A state plan could provide the framework under which a range of state agencies—departments of community affairs, manpower services, business development, energy, transportation, agriculture, human services, education, welfare—could work toward development goals they could not achieve alone. The Massachusetts and California cases demonstrate that state planning can be used to give direction to economic development at the state level.

For planning to achieve its full potential, however, both planners and governors must be willing to change their roles in the planning process. Planners must develop a better understanding of how the private marketplace functions and an ability to be flexible and practical in the "real world" of development economics. Governors must pay more attention to the hundred or more functional plans—mostly mandated by the federal government—which guide the actions of their agencies. Governors must also be willing to play the role of negotiator to see that useful compromises are reached when conflicts arise among the plans put forward by various state agencies. With these changes in approach, planning could begin to provide a much needed central focus for state economic development activities.

5
PEOPLE AND PLACES
WITH SPECIAL NEEDS

No state is without areas that cry out for special attention from economic development architects: the poverty-entrenched rural county, the declining core city, the sprawl-ridden suburb, the environmentally-delicate coastal zone.

Yet the majority of state officials appear to consider it beyond their power and purview to guide development to needy areas and restrict it in "super-heated" localities.

■ Dick Seaman, Wisconsin Development Office: "We would lose our credibility with business. Industry goes where it wishes, based on its own criteria."

■ Governor George Busbee, Georgia: "Any large prospect has consulting firms, siting engineers. They make the decisions."

■ Dick Brock, Florida Bureau of Trade Development: "We try to guide them to where we think they will be most economically successful, rather than to where we think the social needs are paramount."

This prevailing view—that industry goes where it wants and government's only role is to help industry implement its decisions—is open to serious challenge. State governance, constitutionally and politically, should be for a wide constituency—not industry alone. The welfare of citizens and communities, not the convenience of industry, would seem to be the appropriate priority. The object of state policy should be to influence business goals so that they coincide with those of citizens and communities and address the very real social problems which afflict distressed rural, urban and suburban areas alike. And where private and public goals are too divergent, states ought to consider intervening selectively in the private marketplace to fill the cracks through which fall so many people and places.

Potentially one of the most effective state strategies to help people and places with special needs is "targeting." The state identifies—or "tags"—certain regions, residents or economic activities it wishes to assist, then directs state actions—fiscal, regulatory, and, particularly, expenditure policies—toward the "targets." When used in a concerted, well-planned manner, targeting can help bring needy people and places up to parity with the rest of the state and improve their potential for future economic growth.

Among its advantages, targeting, especially of expenditure policies, can begin to improve conditions relatively quickly. Some targeting actions, such as directing state procurements to certain areas or businesses, may be implemented by executive order alone, although successful implementation of a broad targeting strategy requires close cooperation between executive and legislative branches. Also, targeting may help reduce the possibility that state fiscal, regulatory or expenditure policies will have unexpected and undesired side effects.

Every state has some programs which are targeted, but comprehensive targeting as an overall economic development strategy is only now emerging. The premiere example of state targeting policy to date was the much-publicized Massachusetts strategy to preserve cities, neighborhoods and town centers.

The strategy was developed during the administration of former Governor Michael Dukakis from the "bottom up," by a seven-member economic development cabinet working with more than 5,000 officials from 330 Massachusetts cities and towns. It had as its major goals:

■ To revitalize community and regional centers through the redirection of state and federal resources in support of local center revitalization programs;
■ To stabilize the physical, social and economic vitality of neighborhoods through efforts to combat the problems of redlining, housing deterioration, deficient public services, and arson;
■ To promote the maintenance, rehabilitation and reuse of existing buildings through revision of the state building code;
■ To stimulate growth in the state's economy so as to assure sufficient job opportunities for residents;
■ To preserve farmland and protect wetlands; and
■ To decrease dependence on the property tax.

To implement the strategy, the state "targeted" its own facilities and offices to downtown locations, shifted sewer assistance programs to favor densely settled areas ("away from sewering cornfields," as Dukakis put it), diverted state and federal highway funds from new projects in the open countryside to bricking sidewalks and improving city roads. After a heated battle with the education bureaucracy, state school building assistance policy was shifted to favor rehabilitation of schools in center cities rather than abandoning the old structures and forcing cities to build afresh on their outskirts. Three-quarters of the federal park money flowing into the state was directed to major urban centers, almost twice as much as they had received before.

The word went out to industries and developers from Frank Keefe, then head of the Office of State Planning, the lead agency in the development cabinet: "We'll bust our backsides to help you develop in a city industrial park, to rehabilitate an old mill building, to engage in a downtown recycling project. But it's counterproductive for us to spend money extending a sewer line or highway to your development out in the middle of nowhere."

Although most of the strategy involved changes in state expenditure policies, fiscal actions were taken as well. A program providing a state tax credit to companies locating in communities with high local property taxes was amended to apply to expansions of existing businesses, not just new industrial plants, and to cover commercial as well as industrial facilities. Revenue bond financing, previously limited to industrial projects only, was extended to commercial projects in locally designated "commercial area revitalization districts." To help relieve local reliance on property taxes, the state made revisions in the school aid formula and assumed the administrative and financial responsibility for the county court system.

A series of laws was enacted to facilitate financing for and creation of new jobs. Established were:

■ The Massachusetts Capital Resource Company to provide venture capital loans to private businesses in the state, funded by in-state insurance companies;
■ The Technology Development Corporation to provide technical assistance and start-up capital to small, innovative technology-based businesses;
■ The Massachusetts Industrial Finance Agency to consolidate many existing functions and improve the industrial revenue bond process; and
■ The Community Economic Development Assistance Corporation to provide technical assistance to neighborhood redevelopment organizations in their efforts to revitalize communities and promote job creation.

Regulatory changes were also proposed in the strategy. Legislation was introduced, though not enacted, to allow communities to establish review systems to streamline certain local permitting procedures.

As best it could, the state stuck to its strategy. A hot dispute broke out over a major shopping complex for western Massachusetts—whether it should go into downtown Pittsfield, the region's largest city, or on the periphery of a much smaller town, Lenox, endangering the commercial core of the larger city. The state came down four-square for Pittsfield. Dukakis' message to the would-be Lenox developer was:

"There will be no access to the state highway. Forget about your development. We just won't permit it."

Administratively, the centerpiece of the Massachusetts strategy was the development cabinet, headed by the state planning director and staffed by his office, and including the lieutenant governor and secretaries of transportation, economic, community and environmental affairs. This cabinet group met weekly to work on specific economic development programs (ranging from urban parks and housing to retail areas) in the state's economically depressed cities and towns. The goal, often but not consistently achieved, was for the development cabinet to work closely with each city's political and business leadership, urging local leaders to develop jointly with the state a local economic revival plan that the state could back with its specific fiscal, regulatory and expenditure actions, both with its own resources and with state-controlled, federally-funded programs.

A development cabinet would not necessarily suit all other states' political or social cultures. But its creation by a governor who granted it enormous powers and backed its decisions underscores the vital ingredient in all efforts to aid areas of special need: commitment of a state's chief executive. Indeed, without strong central executive guidance and control, any program targeted to distressed areas can easily turn out to be more window dressing than reality. The natural tendency of competing state departments, each with their own constituencies and agendas, is to drift off in their customary direction and to undercut the sharp targeting of efforts required to make a state government operate with full efficiency. Only strong gubernatorial leadership can counteract that trend.

A danger in ambitious programs such as the Massachusetts urban strategy is that the program may be discontinued altogether or momentum lost with the accession of a new state administration. Thus the future of the Massachusetts initiative was uncertain as Dukakis left office in early 1979, although a number of the administrative and legislative changes were likely to remain.

The problems of coordinating and implementing a targeting strategy in the presence of a hydra-headed bureaucracy may seem easy compared to the enormous political hurdles of enacting one. Opposition from legislators and other political forces from outside the targeted communities can doom even the soundest strategy by killing essential pieces of it or by forcing proponents to expand the list of eligible recipients so broadly as to nullify the whole concept of "special" state assistance.

In states where comprehensive targeting is politically impossible, chief executives may want to examine more limited targeted actions that can be undertaken administratively or will more likely be accepted ***33***

The problems of coordinating and implementing a targeting strategy in the presence of a hydra-headed bureaucracy may seem easy compared to the enormous political hurdles of enacting one.

by the legislature.

"In Colorado," says Governor Lamm, "we have two major problems—urban sprawl and rural decay. And it cannot go unobserved that those are twin sides of the same coin."

The Denver metropolitan area in particular continues to experience what Lamm terms "cancerous growth" in population, industries, and energy—and land-consumptive subdivisions. Denver's air pollution, according to some analyses, is the worst in the nation, symbolized by an ugly brown cloud hanging over the city many days of the year. Yet while Denver is booming, census figures show that between 1960 and 1970, 32 of Colorado's 63 counties *lost* population. Though not uniform, rural deprivation is very real in some sections of the state. "People get out of high school in Akron, Colorado, and the San Luis Valley, or in the eastern plains or in Pueblo; they can't find a job there, so they have to move to Denver," Lamm comments. "This drains the resources from rural Colorado and adds to the management problems we have in urban Colorado."

Gaining legislative approval of a conscious plan to steer new growth to rural Colorado has proven impossible. The Denver Chamber of Commerce and similar forces put up the argument "you're trying to tell people where to live" and thereby kill the effort, Lamm claims. The very idea of planning doesn't sit well in his region of the country anyway. Lamm notes: "Planning out in the West is a cowboy getting his Saturday night liquor on Friday night."

Administratively, Lamm's administration has done what it can. "We now spend 70 percent of our time in economic development on where 10 percent of the people live"—in rural areas, Lamm says. The stated goal, says Russell Caldwell, the state's economic development director, is to promote "diversity and stability." Interested industries are told: "We want to give you our services and our information. We want to show you the regions of this state. We want to tell you that while our economy is outperforming that of other states, we have an employment problem. We want to make sure that jobs go to unemployed Coloradoans," Caldwell says. He personally gives major attention to the San Luis Valley, which has Colorado's highest concentration of minority (Hispanic) unemployment. And to influence the flow of federal development dollars toward needy locations,

Caldwell instituted monthly meetings with the three lead agencies he works with at the federal level—the Economic Development Administration, Farmers Home Administration, and Small Business Administration. ("The A-95 review process is not good enough focus," Caldwell asserts.) The net result, he says, is "an informal targeting mechanism" on important development projects. (Similar information coordination between state and federal officials exists in a number of other states, including South Carolina.)

One useful economic development mechanism that in many states could be instituted by administrative action alone is the targeting of state procurements—those goods and services the state purchases from the private sector. State governments are large consumers, buying everything from pencils and paperclips to the services of contractors who construct million dollar public works projects. Some states, as will be discussed in the next chapter, through legislation or administrative order require that a fixed percentage of their procurements be obtained from in-state businesses or small firms. Procurement set-asides could also be applied to minority businesses, as President Carter has done by executive order as part of his 1978 urban policy package, or could require that some goods and services be purchased from firms located in distressed areas.

A major advantage of using targeted procurements as an economic development tool is that their impact can be seen in the short and mid-term. The effects of such a policy are also somewhat easier to control and predict than changes in fiscal, tax or regulatory policies, and procurement set-asides can be used to help encourage other sorts of behavior, such as anti-discrimination. But despite their advantages, procurement policies alone cannot solve serious economic development problems in distressed urban and rural areas. They need to be supplemented with other targeted policies.

Two examples of targeting in Texas and North Carolina show how a less-than-comprehensive strategy can still be a valuable tool in economic development.

In 1973, the Texas legislature created the South Texas Cultural Basin Commission to deal with the chronic poverty of South Texas, a 40-county region as big as Pennsylvania with incomes far below national averages and one-third of its two million residents (half are Hispanic) on welfare. The Commission is seeking to combine and coordinate federal, state, local and private funds to build the region's capital resources and improve schools, public facilities, health care, and transportation. Members include the Governor (chairman), five local citizens, the chairmen of five regional councils of governments, six state agency directors, and the regional directors of five federal agencies. They meet four times a year to make and accept grants, plan **35** and implement programs.

North Carolina state officials have begun a unique and important effort to coordinate state and federal actions, across a rather broad front, to steer economic development to rural areas of special need.

In September 1978, the White House announced it was taking steps to ensure that the actions of three federal agencies, involving more than a billion dollars in federal funds to North Carolina, would be made more consistent with the state's goal of boosting development in rural areas with high poverty and unemployment and inadequate community facilities and services. The agreement may well have marked the first time the federal government had formally recognized the importance of using its public investment programs to support state and local objectives.

Involved were the Farmers Home Administration, which provided $500,000 in grants and loans for rural development, the Department of Housing and Urban Development, which funded a demonstration project to study the problems rural communities face in obtaining federal housing and community development resources, and the Department of Labor, which agreed to collaborate with the state in the $115 million it provides for rural areas in North Carolina. Under this agreement, signed by Governor James Hunt, the state established a rural development coordinating committee, comprised of state and federal representatives, to oversee funding coordination.

6

ENCOURAGING SMALL BUSINESS

Officially every state promotes small business. Indeed, almost all elected officials and candidates for office routinely extol the virtues of the small entrepreneur who turns an innovative idea into a thriving business. Politicians also criticize government for making it too difficult to start a new business today.

But when compared with other state economic development efforts, assistance to small business turns out to be little more than lip service. Small business programs are rarely—if ever—granted the same resources as pursuing outside corporations or retaining big industry in the state. Most programs to assist small business rely heavily on federal funding and inspiration and usually serve a narrow, minority constituency rather than a wide range of entrepreneurs. As one economic development officer told us off the record, "Because we operate in a political world, we have to at least appear to be doing something for small business. But we don't devote a lot of resources to small business. They're just going to have to get up to 50 employees and become a significant employer before we add them to our major efforts."

There are several reasons why state development officials find it difficult to help small business:

■ Small businesses are usually tied to the city where the entrepreneur lives, making one state economic development office located in the state capital of little use to most small businesses in the state.

■ Economic development programs are usually judged on the number of jobs they create, and it is easier to attract—and to document—a few large plants that employ several hundred people than a multitude of small enterprises employing just a few (perhaps only the owner's family).

■ It is difficult to figure out how to help small business. When a small business operator asks for state assistance, he or she usually needs specific technical aid that requires sophisticated expertise beyond the capacity of many state economic development staffs.

■ Helping individual small businesses is relatively expensive and risky. The high failure rate of beginning enterprises—and the potential for short-term job creation followed by sudden unemployment—makes **37** large expenditures of state funds questionable.

Even experienced small business consultants acknowledge that the road to assisting small business is rocky. If resources are limited, cautions John Sower of the non-profit National Development Council, states should probably work only with businesses that have made it through the first year when so many fail.

The reasons for the low-scale state effort may go far deeper, however. By their very nature, beginning entrepreneurs and small business operators who pride themselves on their independence are poorly-organized politically. They have demanded little of state government, except exemptions from regulation and abatement of taxes. Political leaders, meanwhile, have responded to other groups demanding environmental, health and safety regulations that have noble goals but make the business world more expensive and complicated to enter. Some lobbying groups have shown an absolute disdain for small businesses' complaint that they canot afford environmental clean-up costs and high wage rates.

The time may have come, however, for politicians of all viewpoints to come together in support of small business for its unique contribution to the country. Developing new innovative enterprises is obviously important to the nation's economic and social future. Helping new businesses with strong potential is also more effective in the long run than shoring up declining businesses that may require permanent subsidies.

The services performed by state economic development offices are more important to small businesses than large firms, which can afford consultants to help them select sites for new plants or advise them on new markets. "Coca Cola has much more information than we have," noted Dick Brock of Florida. Unfortunately, Brock added, "The small ladies lingerie company run by a man from the East Side of New York with his wife's brother who wants to move to Hialeah and make bras and panties doesn't even know about us."

The climate for small business also plays an important role in job creation and patterns of business ownership. As noted earlier in this paper, David Birch of MIT has found that most new jobs are created by the expansion of existing firms and the birth of new enterprises, and that the Northeastern and Midwestern regions of the country with the lowest rate of new enterprise development also have the slowest rates of employment growth. But the need to encourage small business is no less great in the boomtown atmosphere of the Rocky Mountain West, Colorado's Roy Romer said. The West's traditional pattern of broad ownership of land, housing, and the means of production, Romer said,

is jeopardized today by increasing governmental regulation, tax laws that encourage large companies to acquire small ones, and, as the population ages, the increasing amount of capital placed in conservatively-invested pension funds. Pension funds, noted Romer, are sent out of the state to be managed by the nation's largest banks, which find it easier and safer to invest in skyscrapers in downtown Denver than in small businesses in the state's energy boomtowns and agricultural trading centers. And as the boomtowns grow, he noted, chain stores often have easier access to capital than the longtime local businesses which want to expand to take advantage of the growing economic base. "I'm not an isolationist," Romer said, "but there is something healthy about broad-based ownership and local ownership."

Given the risks involved and small business's preference for an arms-length relationship with the government, the question is how best can the states proceed to alleviate management, capital and regulatory problems?

Since no state has a strong, comprehensive program of assisting small business, a variety of experiences and models and some fresh, untried ideas must be explored.

Most business analysts agree that access to capital is one of the most crucial problems facing small business, if not the most crucial. The problem is not limited to failing businesses or declining areas. Even growing, profitable firms have inadequate access to equity and long-term debt. The reasons are several: Smaller firms have fewer assets to mortgage. Banks traditionally have required smaller firms to pay higher interest rates than their "prime" customers. In declining areas, industries have been "redlined" by banking policies that require higher interests and allow only shorter-term loans.

Several states have developed institutions to provide long-term debt for business expansions, venture capital for new businesses, and technical support for small business. These include the Connecticut Development Authority (CDA), the Massachusetts Industrial Finance Agency (MIFA), the Pennsylvania Industrial Development Authority (PIDA), the Bank of North Dakota, the Alaska Commercial Fisheries and Agricultural Bank and the New Jersey Economic Development Authority.

The Connecticut and Massachusetts programs operate "umbrella" revenue bonds. Under this system, several projects are financed via one public bond issue, thus spreading the risk among several ventures. "Umbrella" bonds are more effective for beginning businesses than self-sustaining industry revenue bonds, which require that the credit of the borrowing firm be strong enough to pay back the loan.

Pennsylvania's program provides second mortgages to firms that have obtained a first mortgage of about 50 percent on a project. The **39**

Bank of North Dakota, the only state-owned bank in the United States, acts as a "banker's bank" by buying up loans that commercial banks have already made. The capital supplies in localities are then replenished.

The Connecticut Product Development Corporation provides "venture capital" for small businesses wishing to develop products "new" to the state. Since 1975, the state has invested approximately $1.3 million in joint ventures with 18 Connecticut companies. The Product Development Corporation provides up to 60 percent of the risk capital costs associated with the development of a specific product or device. If the product is successfully developed and marketed, then the Product Development Corporation receives a royalty on product sales, usually 5 percent.

The Massachusetts Community Development Finance Corporation makes equity investments in and provides long-term debt to community development corporation-controlled business ventures in areas of "substantial" unemployment and economic depression. The Massachusetts program also requires that ventures receiving CDFC assistance create full-time, year-round employment that pays at least 150 percent of the prevailing minimum wage and offers adequate fringe benefits including health insurance.

One way to increase the availability of debt capital to small business is to encourage banks to establish a "two-tier" interest rate program, with a lower rate for small businesses. This sytem was pioneered by Pittsburgh's Mellon Bank in 1977 when interest rates were climbing. Banks in New York, Massachusetts and the District of Columbia followed. States which have set conditions on banks for the deposit of state funds (such as loans to minorities or women or community reinvestment) might add the two-tier interest rate system to their list.

A number of states also offer technical and management assistance to small business. Perhaps the most innovative is the Massachusetts Community Economic Development Assistance Corporation, which helps new enterprises obtain management assistance when they are not eligible for other state programs. Michigan disseminates information to small business operators by sponsoring a lecture series through the state's community college system. "We prepare the curriculum and find suitable lecturers because we feel we have a better handle on what is useful to business than an academic has," said Norton Birman of the Office of Economic Expansion.

A number of states are attempting to improve the climate for small business by using the state's purchasing power to provide small operators the guaranteed markets they may need for stability. Minnesota, Tennessee, Massachusetts and Illinois require state agencies

to buy 5 to 10 percent of their goods and services from the state's small

Helping new businesses with strong potential is . . .
more effective in the long run than shoring up declining
businesses that may require permanent subsidies.

businesses, usually identified as having fewer than 25 employees for retailing and fewer than 50 for manufacturing, with gross sales averaging less than $2 million per year. California also favors small firms, not through a fixed set-aside, but by giving them a 5 percent bidding preference. If a small business's competitive bid on a project comes within 5 percent of the lowest bidder, which is not a small business, the small firm is awarded the contract.

Setting up a worthwhile program to advise small business is a tough business, warns Alex Dingee of Venture Founders, a Massachusetts firm that conducts workshops for potential entrepreneurs and also advises the Canadian province of Nova Scotia on economic development. Businessmen, he said, are often reluctant to share confidential information with a state agency out of fear that the information will be relayed to competitors or other state agencies. Business operators would have to be assured that access to their records would be strictly limited.

State technical assistance programs could also serve the purpose of bringing together entrepreneurs and local residents with venture capital, Dingee notes. Just the publicity that entrepreneurs are looking for capital sometimes shakes loose private money, he added.

In recent years, several states have begun programs to promote small business manufactured goods and agricultural products both domestically and internationally. West Virginia, for example, has created seven state-supervised farmer's markets, designed to aid farmers by giving them a place to market their goods. The markets also give wholesale buyers and merchants, as well as consumers, an excellent source of home-grown products. They could also be a part of a downtown revitalization strategy in medium and larger sized cities. In 1976, more than $2 million worth of produce was sold through West Virginia's state markets.

Other states have joined together, through the federal regional commissions, to hire farming specialists—both foreign and domestic—to promote their agricultural products. A more extensive survey of foreign promotion is covered in Chapter 6.

To help small business wade through state regulation, a number of states have established "ombudsmen" who can explain which agency grants which permit and present the case of small operators who have trouble with the bureaucracy. California's economic development office, for example, sets up meetings between businessmen and state **41** agencies. "We're not reducing standards, but there are different ways to do things at an early stage," said Alan Stine, Secretary of Business and Transportation. The meetings and cooperation among agencies often amaze business executives who have read that California is a difficult state to do business with, noted Betty Bryant, the state's Economic Development Director. "When I told a company we could speed up the review of their Environmental Impact Review to 30 days, they were so impressed they got this glassy-eyed look and went out the door."

In a state with strong regulatory bodies, small businesses especially need assistance in presenting their case before state agencies, noted Dick Davis of the San Diego Economic Development Commission. His organization has represented San Diego businesses before the California Coastal Zone Commission.

California's economic development department has also assisted the state's Occupational Safety and Health Administration in getting information on new rules to small businesses.

Small business groups themselves have won many exemptions from government regulation. Whether more exemptions are warranted—or even whether current exemptions are appropriate—is beyond the scope of this paper. As part of improved economic analysis, however, the states might re-examine their regulatory policies to determine whether small business is suffering needlessly under regulations that are either poorly designed or set up primarily to control larger industries.

Finally, the states could also assist small businesses by encouraging efforts begun by localities and the private sector to improve business conditions. This could be accomplished through direct funding of metropolitan business development authorities or incentives to encourage localities and private groups to move in certain directions. One of the most interesting, unproven concepts is the new City Venture Corporation, formed by Control Data Corporation, the Minneapolis Star and Tribune Company, and Bertrand Goldberg Associates of Chicago, to "plan and manage" implementation of innovative and comprehensive inner city projects by marketing the corporation's services to communities, cities, states and federal agencies, and where appropriate, to invest in private business opportunities related to urban development. The City Venture approach grows out of Control Data's conviction that there are sound business opportunities in what others regard as ravaged city areas, and that "comprehensive" rather than piecemeal solutions are required for inner city problems.

However difficult to implement, state assistance for small businesses should receive high priority because: (1) this is the area in which most new jobs are created in the economy, and (2) the assistance usually goes to a state's own citizen-entrepreneurs for locally generated activity in which the return on investment will be realized within the state, not by distant stockholders. Efficiently implemented, state efforts in this area should prove to be as wise politically as they are economically.

7
MANPOWER TRAINING

The United States has one of the worst records of any industrialized nation in relating the world of education to the world of work, former Labor Secretary Willard Wirtz once noted. Despite literally billions of federal, state, local and private dollars funneled each year into job training, high unemployment and underemployment abound.

Especially hard hit are the young, black, brown and female, who constitute over half of the unemployed in the nation today. At the same time, many with good educations—from the highly trained Ph.D. to the young teacher to the skilled mechanic—cannot find suitable work in their field of expertise. Somewhere, somehow, our labor systems have failed us.

The problems run so deep that it is clear job training bears only a small part of the blame. In many states, persistent unemployment problems result from either inadequate job growth or uneven distribution of jobs which do exist. Structural as well as social barriers create significant employment problems for minorities and the disadvantaged.

Moreover, a job is not always a job. Some jobs are sufficiently stable and well-paying to allow people to support their families, pay their taxes and avoid welfare and unemployment insurance. Others are not. To distinguish between these two kinds of jobs, economists have recently developed the theory of the "dual labor market." Primary labor market jobs pay adequate wages and benefits, require or teach job skills, and are organized into internal promotion ladders that offer the worker a chance for upward mobility. Families can generally be supported on the wages of a primary labor market job. Secondary labor market jobs, on the otherhand, are usually low-paying—often at the poverty level—provide few benefits, require or impart few skills, are seldom unionized and tend to involve high repetitive tasks. Workers in the secondary labor market are often unable to support their families on the basis of earnings alone. Millions of these workers have turned to government programs for supplemental assistance; still others have turned to illegal activities to support themselves and their families.

Obviously, improving state job training efforts alone will not resolve these serious labor market problems. The single most effective employment strategy is a strong economy. Earlier chapters in this paper have touched on measures to improve overall economic and employment climates in the states—by expanding the state's rate of job growth through policies which target resources to areas or residents in greatest distress, promote new and small enterprises, and nurture a relationship between the public and private sectors to build job-creating, community-based enterprises. Without these measures, even the best job training program will have only very limited impact.

Job training programs can, however, play an important role in supporting a state's overall economic development strategy. Job training can be one more element of public expenditure policy that is targeted to small businesses, distressed areas, minority residents or other state economic development priorities. It can be a vehicle to help residents move from unemployment to jobs, from secondary to primary labor market employment.

In fact, a number of states are already using job training as part of a strategy to attract large industry. In recent years, programs have been instituted to provide made-to-order workforces, at state expenses, for industries which agree to locate or expand in the state. Critics may rightly throw darts at a strategy skewed toward large industry. (These programs are not having much impact in combatting broad structural unemployment.) Nevertheless, the programs do provide a good example of how a job training program can "fit" into the state development strategy.

A prerequisite to fitting job training programs into an economic development strategy—a step that must be taken before most states could even begin effective targeting—is to take stock of the many programs which already exist and try to coordinate them better. One must first consider, for instance, the lack of program integration and the sheer complexity of the federal-state employment security and training systems. One state has 11 separate job training programs, each with an annual appropriation of $10 million or more, administered by the federal government, 12 state departments and agencies and at least seven local agencies. For one client group with special problems—offenders—10 state agencies and boards were providing related, but often uncoordinated, employment training.

"The federally-funded manpower programs, state-funded community colleges, and vocational high schools, various local skill centers and private institutions—we've got to get it organized," said the state's former commerce director. "We don't agree on what our respective turfs are. We don't have common planning cycles. We hardly talk to employers. We're just busy doing our own little thing in a vacuum. And we count our successes in terms of the number of graduates of our programs, which is not to be confused with the numbers that get jobs in their chosen fields."

For some states, consolidation of job training and related programs **45**

... a job is not always a job. Some jobs are sufficiently stable and well-paying to allow people to support their families, pay their taxes and avoid welfare and unemployment insurance. Others are not.

into a single state agency may be the most effective way to improve their efficiency. The department might include, for example, industrial training programs, the state employment and training council, the Comprehensive Employment and Training Act (CETA) balance-of-state prime sponsor, the employment security office, and a small research and program development staff to develop innovative and effective uses of funds (such as the governor's 4 percent CETA discretionary monies) and to coordinate joint training programs with private sector participants.

Consolidating employment and training activities in a single agency may be at best a long-term goal for many states. But chief executives can implement incremental mechanisms to improve coordination. A governor can, for example, promote the development of a statewide occupational information network to assure training programs are allocating their resources toward occupations for which there is and will be genuine demand. Massachusetts has formed such a device, the Massachusetts Occupational Information Coordinating Committee, to combine the information resources of eight state agencies for use by state and local officials in designing employment training programs.

The governor's CETA discretionary monies can provide a source of funds to promote coordination, and could be used, for example, to create mechanisms to facilitate data exchange, synchronize planning and funding cycles among job training programs, promote cooperative agreements between federal, state and local and private training agencies to minimize duplication, and realign service delivery systems so that some geographic areas or classes of recipients are not overserved while others are neglected.

One state exhibiting a high degree of coordination in its job training activities is South Carolina. The state Technical and Comprehensive Education program (TEC), begun 17 years ago to ease the transition from a society dominated by cotton, tobacco and textiles to a multifaceted industrial economy, has expanded to 16 technical colleges (and 55 vocational high schools), scattered throughout the state, each reflecting the economic climate of its region. (The colleges are located so that almost none of the 125,000 TEC students must commute more than one half hour.)

46   The Board is an independent state agency, not within the

department of education or commerce, and answerable on its own to the governor and legislature. It is carefully integrated, however, with other state programs and agencies whose activities bear on technical education and vocational training. The Director of the State Development Board, for example, serves on TEC's advisory panel, as does the Superintendent of Education. TEC is the prime subcontractor for all vocational training under CETA—the governor is the sole prime sponsor—making South Carolina the only state with one prime sponsor and one agency exclusively responsible for all institutional training. TEC also runs the state's "Special Schools" program to train workers for incoming or expanding industries.

In addition to the lack of coordination among states and federal job training programs, public programs frequently fail to involve effectively the private sector, which has at least 80 percent of the nation's jobs. In most states, the services and advice of private employers—both as advisors to state job training programs and as direct participants in joint programs—are underutilized.

"Greater reliance on the private sector will not be easy to achieve," says the Committee for Economic Development, a nonprofit business-oriented research organization. Factors contributing to lagging private support, the group says, include "concern that these activities [impose] an undue burden on the firm's regular profit-making operations, disappointments with particular program results, and impatience with the red tape and lack of stability in funding and management frequently connected with federally assisted private programs."

There are examples around the country of private sector participation improving the relevance and impact of job training programs. The success of Wisconsin's 69-year old vocational education program, widely regarded as one of the country's best, is largely due to its close association with representatives from the business and labor sectors, according to Fred Hiestand, Assistant Director of Vocational, Technical and Adult Education. "Organized labor plays a very heavy role in governing vocational education schools at the state and local level," he said, "but we have management representatives that act as a built-in counterforce." Wisconsin's 16 regional technical institutes are each governed by a board with employee and employer membership. An overseeing state board is similarly structured, with three employer members, three employees, three farmers and three ex-officio representatives. A network of 1,500 - 2,000 advisory board members help design the curriculum. "They make very specific recommendations on the kind of equipment Wisconsin companies will be using and what we should train on," Hiestand explained.

There are also some good examples around the country of private **47** sector involvement directly in the training of workers. The Chicago Alliance of Business Manpower Services (CABMS), a private non-profit organization to attack the city's worst job problems, was formed by 20 large Chicago companies in alliance with 20 minority firms. The group's permanent staff acts as a direct contractor for federally financed manpower programs, and currently handles all of Chicago's federally supported on-the-job training (OJT) contracts with private and nonprofit employers. OJT, the mainstay of Title I of CETA, provides publicly financed training and work experience in a setting where private employers have guaranteed work for successful trainees. Nevertheless, most OJT programs do not effectively use employer expertise and resources to train participants.

"[CABMS] has been unusually innovative and effective in carrying out a wide variety of activities designed to serve the training and employment needs of marginal groups in the labor force," writes the Committee for Economic Development in *Jobs for the Hard-to-Employ.* "By making direct use of business experience, expertise and innovation, this arrangement has led to a sharp reduction in the delays and red tape previously involved in awarding OJT contracts, costs of training programs have been cut significantly, a large number of subcontractors (particularly smaller firms) have been brought into the OJT effort, and various innovative approaches to job placement have been developed," the report says.

Once job training programs are better coordinated and integrated with the private sector, states can begin to use them effectively as tools of state economic development policy. A state goal of expanding primary labor market opportunities for its residents would necessarily involve a wide variety of fiscal, regulatory and expenditure policies designed to create and nurture such employment. Job training programs, as a form of public expenditure policy, would be supportive of the overall goal.

One excellent state strategy would target resources toward community-based economic development, particularly the assistance of small enterprises that offer the possibility of increased primary labor market jobs. Job training programs might be used to help supply a trained workforce to new, small firms, giving them an edge up until their operations reach full capacity. The various CETA programs—in particular the Titles providing classroom training, support services, work experience and on-the-job training—could be partly used to train managers to run small firms or community-based enterprises. CETA's public sector employment program could help support needed community services and infrastructure projects in areas to which state policies are targeted.

48   The governor's CETA discretionary funds could also support a

community development strategy. Massachusetts, for example, inaugurated during the summer of 1976 the Massachusetts Local Initiative Program (MLIP), funded with CETA discretionary money, to assist community-based organizations in providing services and employment in their localities. MLIP awarded about $1 million to 27 community groups and local government sponsors (300 applications were submitted) for a wide range of projects: training mildly retarded adults to serve as teachers' aides for retarded youngsters, establishing a cultural center for a Portuguese-speaking community in the southeastern part of the state, aiding the Wampanoag Tribal Council and the Worcester Tenants' Association. Overall, nearly 300 jobs were created. Although support was withdrawn after six months, several projects proved commercially viable, including a community canning center, a fishery and a food cooperative. Even for those projects that did not continue, MLIP helped teach new job skills, provide work experience, and boost community organizations. The MLIP program did have disadvantages, however. Too few jobs were primary sector, and only a few projects achieved self-sufficiency. It might be an ideal type of program to help stabilize employment in areas afflicted with business or seasonal cyclical downturns, but would not have much impact on structural unemployment problems. One major advantage from the chief executive's point of view, of course, is that the program can be implemented by executive action alone.

An ideal state development strategy would also include job training programs to ensure residents are prepared to meet any increase in demand for primary labor market employment. In addition to classroom instruction, the job program might emphasize apprenticeship and on-the-job training. Apprenticeships pay relatively low wages and offer few benefits, but they do provide excellent skill training and access to primary markets through informal contacts with potential future employers. An apprenticeship element is already a key feature of some state vocational programs, notably Wisconsin's, which is based on the old European model of training.

Even though the principal focus of the ideal state strategy would be community-based development, some states might wish to continue programs of industrial training for incoming or expanding industries. While these touch only a fraction of the workforce and should in no way substitute for broader based programs, they do have some important advantages. They train workers for "known" jobs, in cooperation with private industry. Moreover, these programs use state agencies and state personnel to select and screen trainees, frequently in cooperation with the state's employment security commission. This enables the state to "target" the participants, making sure, for example, that minority and other needy residents get a shot at jobs **49** they may not know about or qualify for if private industry alone makes the selection.

The state training strategy would include special programs targeted to traditionally hard-to-employ residents. One relatively new approach appears to be having preliminary success in breaking the "welfare" orientation of most current programs for these clients. The Manpower Demonstration Research Corporation (MDRC), a nonprofit organization funded with private and public dollars, oversees 13 supported work programs around the country, employing about 2,000 workers. Clients include ex-offenders, ex-addicts, welfare mothers and low-income minority youths. They are given partially subsidized jobs (hence the term "supported work") in the public and private sector. The Pivot Corporation in Seattle, for example, has since 1975 trained its clients in the field of furniture manufacturing, construction and renovation and parks maintenance. Although primarily supported with federal and foundation funds, Pivot operates like a "real" business. Its board of directors is composed of 11 local business people (including a representative from Boeing), and the enterprise is expected to become self-sufficient, since MDRC funds will eventually cease. Over 650 trainees have completed Pivot's 12-month program. About one-third have found permanent jobs.

The strong involvement of the private sector and an orientation toward on-the-job primary labor market training make Pivot's record of job placement for the hard-to-employ, modest as it is, better than most traditional job training programs. Nevertheless, a large pool of structural unemployment remains untapped. No matter how well-connceived and well-implemented a job training program may be, it can be no stronger than the overall economic development strategy of which it is a part.

For states relying on job training alone to solve unemployment and underemployment problems, no amount of funding will be sufficient. Only when targeted in a specific strategy, along with the numerous other resources of state government, can such programs collectively begin to show impressive, cost-effective results.

ECONOMIC ANALYSIS

A prerequisite of state and local governments mobilizing their legal powers and resources to improve their economies, noted University of Missouri political scientist Norton Long, is a "theoretical conceptualization of state and local economies." State officials, Long noted, have much to learn about their territory—"how their people are earning their livings, what is happening to the sources of livelihoods, their industry mix and what is happening to it, investment and disinvestment, the capacity to generate jobs, markets, competition, the skills mix of their labor force and its relationship to the industry mix, wage levels, productivity costs, comparative costs including state and local taxes."

But when businessmen and state officials discuss economic development, said one tax analyst who works with state governments, "it's like a poker game in which the chips are held by one side."

No matter how strong a commitment a state makes to improving its business climate, it rarely conducts good, rigorous research on state economic issues. The result is that neither politicians nor state economic development officers have confidence in their understanding of the state's economy or how best to improve it. They are forced into blind reliance on information produced by outside sources— usually large corporations or banks—whose goals may or may not mesh with the public interest. The lack of basic research results in unimaginative and sometimes misdirected economic development strategies.

"A governor always has plenty of business advice from the chief [business] executives of the state. But he never knows where they're coming from. They all have their own axe to grind," noted one state business economist.

"Most studies of a state's comparative advantages tend to reproduce its existing and frequently inadequate industrial base, rather than identify possible avenues for change," observed Michael Kieschnick, an independent financial economist.

The most obvious reasons for the lack of state-conducted economic research is that it has not been recognized as a necessary activity, and it is hard to get the state legislatures to pay for it. But the reasons may go far deeper—into the preferences of analysts themselves. "Planners and economists have tended to ignore state subjects, preferring the prestige of national policy or the social concerns inherent in urban policy," **51** noted Sandra Kanter, assistant professor of economics at the University of Massachusetts.

But today there is increasing evidence that macroeconomic analyses and federal government economic strategies will not do the job for either old industrial cities or booming areas. Despite the national rebound from the 1974-1975 recession, unemployment rates have continued higher in declining industrial areas while overheated economies in booming regions have fueled inflation and suffered from unruly growth patterns.

State governments need to develop long-term economic policies that may even bring into question long held assumptions about "what's good" for the states, Colorado state treasurer Roy Romer said. "Lots of money is spent on economic studies, but the questions I'm interested in aren't asked," he added.

Too often, Romer continued, states adopt the view that all industrial development is good or that one industry is scarce. In Colorado, "tourism is like motherhood," said Romer (a former ski resort operator). "All we can get is good. But if you're a father with five children, what do you want your kids to do for the rest of their lives? Clean beds?"

State economic development officials, Romer said, should investigate such basic questions as whether new industry creates jobs for state residents or induces in-migration, how government regulation affects patterns of ownership and the social structure of a state. In addition, he believes states, especially in low population regions such as the Rocky Mountains, should find ways to cooperate in regional issues such as airline routes, higher education and technology development.

State economic studies also need to examine the relationship between the states and the private sector in economic development. "There hasn't been sufficient appreciation that when you're in the public sector, you really have to follow the lead of the private sector," Romer said. "You can bend it and direct it, but you can't start it or stop it."

Classically, the most effective critics of any economic system are those who know it the best. State government's job is thus to take full advantage of all the research and analytic capability it can glean or capture from the private sector, even while keeping the public rather than private business interest foremost in its own decision-making and priority-setting.

This may also require innovation in personnel policy. Romer appropriately noted that "there's no way you can duplicate" in government "the expertise that comes from experience" in private economic life. "There's a real danger that if you hired a state

In Colorado, "tourism is like motherhood," said Romer (a former ski resort operator). "All we can get is good. But if you're a father with five children, what do you want your kids to do for the rest of their lives? Clean beds?"

economist, you almost have to have an absolute thing that he couldn't have tenure," Romer suggests. "You just can't work in government and understand how the private sector works and thinks. You've got to have the rotation of people going back and forth. You get terribly provincial and parochial if you stay on the public side of this thing too long. It's those guys [in the private sector] who have an accountability mechanism that won't quit, and that's the bottom line. They go broke if they make mistakes, and they disappear once they do that. On the government side, we get a supplemental appropriation." Thus, says Romer, "You've got to build-in structures that achieve an honest give-and-take between the public and private sectors on fundamental policy."

In contrast to the states' generally abysmal record in economic analysis, California and Florida provide examples of how states could undertake analysis and turn it into economic development strategies.

California's state government took a new interest in economic development following the Dow Chemical Company's decision in 1977 not to build a new plant that would have employed 500 people. Dow cited delays and a lack of cooperation from state government as the major reasons for abandoning 10 years of plans for the project.

In August 1977, the California Assembly created a new Department of Economic and Business Development, including an Office of Economic Planning, Policy and Research. The purpose of the economic analysis unit is to gather and analyze pertinent information useful to industry, commerce and agriculture, and serve as an advisor to the government, the legislature and the business community.

Despite California's size and complicated economy, the resources of the economic analysis unit are so limited that it has been forced to develop a structure and priorities that could be used by much smaller states. Its staff consists of a chief state business economist, three professional economists and a researcher.

The keys to running an economic analysis unit on a limited budget, California chief business economist Andrew Safir said, are to make use of existing information in the state and to set research priorities very carefully.

Safir chose to locate the Office of Economic Planning, Policy and Research in San Francisco to have easy access to the resources of the **53** business community. Instead of trying to collect their own statistics, Safir and his staff borrow from banks, large corporations, consulting firms and other state agencies. The resources that are borrowed more than make up for the cost of office space, which is more expensive in San Francisco's business district than in the state capital of Sacramento where the other divisions of the state's economic development program are located. (States with less sophisticated information bases might request help from the regional Federal Reserve banks to assemble a data base. The current involvement of the Federal Reserve banks in state and regional economic policy varies widely from region to region, and state officials would have to take the initiative in forging this relationship.)

Safir also relies on informal advice from an advisory council of corporate executives, labor and religious leaders, small businessmen and minority spokesmen.

Because of its limited resources, California's economic analysis unit avoids involvements in specific projects and concentrates on statewide and industrywide analysis that can be "multiplied" to serve more people. "My way of ordering priorities is 'what is the economic impact'?" Safir said. "If you get involved in the minutae, you get lost in it. You may do a great job for one company, but you're failing the state." (Other divisions of the state economic development program do help specific businesses, he noted.)

The office regularly issues publications analyzing state economic performance and sectoral development, including the housing market outlook, an analysis of monthly unemployment trends and the consumer price index. In addition, the office puts out occasional papers on such subjects as consumer credit nationwide and specific industry studies on the chemical, auto and aerospace industries. Plans are underway for a quarterly state economic forecast.

The audience is the governor's office, other state agencies and any interested parties in the state, including the business community and the press. Safir encourages other state agencies to consider the economic development implications of their agencies. California's shortage of housing, he explained, concerns the economic development department because employers will not site plants where they cannot find acceptable housing for workers.

Using his own experience working for the Council of Economic Advisors and other federal agencies, Safir also tracks federal legislation that may affect California, particularly in the area of energy policy.

Safir walks a fine line between playing the role of ombudsman for the business community and staying out of political decision-making. **54** The best way to do this, he says, is by sticking to providing the governor with economically-based, rather than politically-based, information. If the state economist is used as a "political point man," Safir said, it detracts from his ability to provide unbiased information and decreases his credibility with the business community.

California's economic research operation is still so young that its impact has not yet been felt to any large degree in the day-to-day program operations of the California state government, other state officials said. Nor has the state's economic research been coordinated with research produced by other state agencies. The presence of economic theorists in state government has been important, however, in developing the governor's understanding of the California economy's relationship to the national and international economies.

Florida's Bureau of Economic Analysis, a division of the state Department of Commerce, provides much more comprehensive analysis and services to localities.

Based upon a comprehensive state economic analysis, for example, the state adopted very specific, quantifiable ten-year (1988) goals:

■ Raise Florida's per capita income from 94.1 percent of the U.S. level in 1976 to 100 percent by 1988.
■ Raise Florida's total labor force participation rate from its 1970 level of 53.4 percent to 56 percent by 1988.
■ Increase Florida's manufacturing employment from 11.3 percent of total wage and salary employment in 1975 to 14 percent by 1988.
■ Increase high-wage manufacturing employment from 33.3 percent of the state's manufacturing employment in 1974 to 50 percent by 1988, reversing the trend of recent years.
■ Increase employment in the finance, insurance and real estate sector from 6.6 percent of total Florida wage and salary employment in 1975 to 9 percent by 1968.
■ Maintain wage and salary income at no less than 48 percent of total personal income in Florida.

Florida's county-by-county economic analysis of potential economic development has been particularly effective and useful, state officials said, in helping less populated counties determine which industries have the greatest potential for development in their region.

Perhaps the most perplexing question now facing state economic analysts is whether to adopt econometric modeling. In the 1970s, the use of econometric modeling in both corporations and the federal government has been spurred by the development of time-sharing computer technology. As *Fortune* magazine has noted, "every major corporation" now uses one or more commercial models to help predict the strength of consumer markets, trends in wage rates and prices of **55** materials. Various federal government agencies have their own models, and many Members of Congress and executive branch officials now consider the models as indispensable tools in decision-making. Other officials in Washington and in the business world complain, however, that models too often disagree, and do not account for such externalities as the Arab oil boycott or some type of disaster which can have a dramatic effect on our economy.

A number of state departments of revenue and finance have started to use econometric models to predict tax revenues. The question now is whether the model can be refined for more creative uses in economic analysis and development policy—and at what price. Some states and federal region 1 commissions have hired nationally recognized econometric modeling firms only to find that they lacked the skilled personnel needed to analyze the information once it reached the state. And one northeastern economic director, with easy access to sophisticated econometric modeling at national universities in his state, told us of "dozens of examples where good things would have been missed" by the econometric modeling approach. "I'm a nuts and bolts pragmatic business type from the real world," he said. "I like to go out and work with what's real and what's there."

Other state economists have high praise for models, however. Robert Milbourne of Wisconsin's Department of Revenue found multiple uses for the sophisticated econometric model the state has built: developing a comprehensive tax reform package for a state tax reform commission, studying a sample of Wisconsin taxpayers to determine the importance of inheritance taxes in outmigration of the elderly, analyzing how farmers are treated by the state tax system, and studying the effect of increased mining and a proposed minerals tax on the state's economy.

California's Safir considers any development operation without access to an econometric model "steering a very blind force. I'm not saying you rely on them to swear by them, but they're a very important tool of the trade in this inexact science."

The biggest drawback to creating an econometric model is cost. Wisconsin spends $75,000 per year, plus staff time, for a large-scale, in-house model. But other states have adopted smaller models that cost less or found ways of piggybacking on models used by the state university system.

It is difficult to reach a final conclusion on whether econometric modeling is worth its cost to the state. Many of the models developed by state universities need time-consuming modification before they can be adapted to the needs of economic development offices, and the
56 cost is always high. But if state officials are to deal with confidence in

the world of economic development, an economic model may be very useful to their program.

9
THE INTERNATIONAL ANGLE

Foreign investment in the United States has expanded at a seemingly exponential rate in the 1970s, uncovering a whole new arena of activity for state economic development departments.

The Commerce Department estimates direct foreign investment in the U.S. (excluding foreign holdings of U.S. securities) has doubled in the past five years and now totals $40 billion or more, compared to $200 billion in U.S. investments abroad. In manufacturing alone, foreign firms announced 274 new U.S. investments in 1977.

Foreign companies now own such all-American nameplates as Brylcreem ("a little dab will do ya"), Pepsodent toothpaste, Nestle's chocolate, Gimbel's and Saks' department stores, Clorox bleach, Alka-Seltzer, Libby's foods, Shell Oil, Kool cigarettes, Grand Union, Foster Grant sunglasses and Bantam books.

In their rush to tap the foreign gold mine, states have pursued two major types of activities: (1) policies to encourage foreign firms to buy or locate in the state (so-called "reverse investment") and (2) programs to help domestic firms in the state, particularly small ones, learn the ins and outs of exporting and trading abroad.

Many states have established overseas offices and embarked on recruitment missions, undertaken expensive port expansions, put together large incentive packages for foreign firms, spent millions to advertise in overseas publications and begun to publish world trade directories and newsletters on their own. But it seems likely that some states are overemphasizing promotion and neglecting creative analysis and research that can reveal what kinds of reverse investment and export assistance will most benefit a state's economy, particularly in generating high quality jobs and filling "gaps" that domestic firms may be unable or unwilling to fill. An environment of fierce inter-state competition is being generated, accompanied by substantial waste of state funds.

Background: From 1959 to 1973, foreign investment in the U.S. grew at an average annual rate of 6.5 percent. It swelled abruptly to over 20 percent in 1973 and 1974, turned down slightly during the recession, and more recently has been approaching earlier growth records.

Why this sudden burst of foreign investment interest in the U.S.? Jane Sneddon Little of the Federal Reserve Bank of Boston suggests that since 1945, European and Japanese firms have been gaining the financial strength and technical expertise necessary for U.S. investment. Many were spurred by the devaluations of the dollar and the relatively inexpensive prices at which American properties became available. The stock market's sharp decline enabled foreign investors to buy shares in U.S. corporations at bargain basement prices. But the major reasons for the growth in foreign investment are long-term confidence in the U.S. as a place to do business, inflation and monetary problems notwithstanding, and a desire to tap the huge American markets.

About one-third of foreign investments are in the manufacturing sector, led by chemicals and drugs, electrical and non-electrical machinery, metals and food. Finance, insurance and real estate rank second in popularity. The most active foreign nations in U.S. investments, according to the Conference Board, a business research organization, are Germany, the United Kingdom, Canada, Japan, France, Switzerland and the Netherlands. Doomsday predictions of a massive Arab takeover have not materialized; most oil-producing nations currently prefer liquid investments in stocks, bonds and short-term government securities. "All they get for that," says *Newsweek,* "is a piece of the national debt and a cushion against the losses they suffer from pricing their oil in dollars." OPEC nations own less than one percent of the foreign investment in American industry.

Indeed, there appears to be little public concern over foreign investment, except perhaps where farmland and other real estate is concerned. In 1977, Congress passed legislation requiring overseas buyers of U.S. farmland to report their purchases to the Agriculture Department. A 1978 report from the General Accounting Office, examining 25 farm counties in California, Georgia, Kansas, Missouri and Oklahoma, found foreign ownership of farmland of about 0.3 percent, mostly by Europeans. No one is sure whether this figure is likely to increase substantially.

Before embarking on recruitment efforts, states would be wise to examine where most reverse investment is occurring, and why. New research from a variety of sources is beginning to indicate that certain areas may have a built-in advantage in attracting overseas investors. For example, despite the popular perception, the lion's share of foreign investments have not gone to the Sunbelt, although this region is doing well, but rather to the Mid-Atlantic and New England states. In only one major category, plant construction per capita, does another region—the Southeast—lead, with New England, the Midwest and Southwest clustered close behind in second place.

The two charts contained in Appendix B, taken from an article by Little in the *New England Economic Review* (July/August 1978), give a general picture of how the states and regions fare in foreign manufacturing investment.

Another important finding, not shown on the charts, is that nearly two-thirds of the value of 1978 foreign manufacturing investment in cities went to distressed cities, according to Conference Board figures for the first three-quarters of last year. (Real estate investment follows the opposite pattern, with two-thirds of the urban investments in non-distressed cities.)

What are some of the major factors influencing foreign investment decisions? Research from Little and others indicates that a large number of foreign investors prefer the acquisition of existing plants to the construction of new ones, giving older regions an advantage. Not only can such plants often be bought at low prices, they also enable the foreign firm to enter the U.S. market relatively quickly. Depressed cities may benefit from their greater abundance of highly skilled labor compared to other areas. This is a major motivation for some foreign firms, particularly the Japanese and Germans who tend to emphasize quality control in production, concludes Robert Cohen of Columbia University.

Contrary to general perceptions, Little discovered that foreign firms are no more or less concerned about labor unions than American corporations. Foreigners do appear more concerned about differentials in state wage rates, and tend to place more emphasis on the availability of good port facilities, she found.

Subjective factors play a role in foreign locational decisions. "It is clear from many selection histories that the reception given to visiting foreigners by state development officials, bankers and even restauranteurs and taxi drivers can be terribly important," Little reported.

In light of the ferocious competition for foreign investment now apparent, it is ironic to note that one of Little's findings was that the number of state development incentives, foreign recruitment missions and overseas offices have only a minor impact on foreign investors' locational decisions. Little believes tax abatements may actually deter some foreign investors who might agree with the sentiment expressed by a Michelin Tire vice president in Greenville, South Carolina, to *Business Week* last year: "Every time there is an inducement, it is usually a counterpoint of something bad, like poorly trained labor, or no labor."

Recruitment missions, overseas offices and attention from high ranking state officials can have diplomatic and public relations value. But excessive state spending in these areas may be foolish. "You don't need a large office in Brussels," suggests David Bauer of the

Conference Board. "That may be a very poor substitute to having two

The number of state development incentives, foreign recruitment missions and overseas offices have only a minor impact on foreign investors' locational decisions.

knowledgeable people greet the foreign visitor when he comes to the state . . . And you don't need 15 people from the governor's staff to go to Paris, London or Brussels. Foreign investors can spot a junket." Latest reports show at least 33 states have offices in Europe and Japan, though many are small, shared with someone else or merely information facilities. Increasing numbers of states are advertising in foreign publications; some have budgets of over $250,000 for this purpose. More than half the states, according to the National Association of State Development Agencies, distribute information overseas about state trade and investment opportunities; at least 17 assist foreign firms in the actual development of trade activities and half or more have officially endorsed foreign missions.

What are the results? When is enough too much? Many of the leading states in foreign manufacturing investment pursue aggressive foreign promotion programs. But California, increasing in popularity to the point where it ranked third in desired location for foreign manufacturing investors in 1977, based on Conference Board data, has, until very recently, done almost nothing at the state level to attract reverse investment.

The "personal touch" may be the most important. A warm, understanding reception for visiting foreign industrialists is essential. "Some states can catch the fish and then don't know what to do with it," Bauer says. States ought to have a person on their economic development staff who understands federal and state laws that may be confusing to overseas investors, especially anti-trust, environmental, anti-discrimination and accounting statutes. "Sometimes development officials get so involved with wage rates that they forget about OSHA and pensions," Bauer observers. Southeastern states, he noted, usually excel in preparing detailed and helpful answers.

A governor's personal role can be important. "The majority of prospects we introduce to the governor are very impressed," says Robert Leak of South Carolina. "Many have never met their own head of state."

Despite the "diplomatic" value of an occasional governor's appearance (a factor some state officials believe important, others not), it would seem excessive for a governor to make several foreign trips annually. One former Southern chief executive traveled with **61** state recruitment officers six weeks per year. "These trips are about 90 percent of the cost and 10 percent of the results," says Florida's Dick Brock.

One measure to encourage overseas investors is the reduction of inventory taxes—those levies on the value of goods still in the company warehouse at the end of the taxable year. Another is the establishment of free trade zones—areas adjacent to a port of entry where firms may store, package, assemble or exhibit imported goods free of U.S. duties, so long as they stay in the zone, are transshipped or exported.

The judgment on free trade zones is mixed. Some of the 40 now located around the country (up from only 10 in 1970) have apparently helped to generate new economic activity or retain firms that considered leaving due to high costs. But too often they have been established without careful planning. One Midwestern city invested $350,000 in creating a zone, according to the *Wall Street Journal,* only to find it is still without clients. Labor unions frequently oppose the zones, claiming they make it easy for U.S. companies to import more parts from abroad at the expense of U.S. jobs. Such companies, they claim, assemble the parts inside the zone and import the finished product at an import duty much lower than the sum of its parts.

Assisting Export and Trade: While excessive recruitment efforts run the risk of wasting state resources, few states would not benefit from a vigorous program to help small and medium-sized firms, otherwise lacking in appropriate contracts and research capability, in locating foreign markets and trade partners for their goods and services.

"Soon after I became Governor," says George Busbee of Georgia, "I discovered through talking to businessmen in my state that an increasing number of small and medium-sized firms, including agricultural concerns, wanted to export, but did not understand the foreign marketplace." Busbee sponsored and the legislature approved in 1977 a law creating the Georgia World Congress Institute for Foreign Trade, a non-profit, state funded institute promoting a cooperative relationship between the state's university system and the private business community to attract foreign investment and expand export markets for state products. Among the services provided are management education and research for small and medium-sized firms, lectures and conferences on issues ranging from accounting to the U.S. construction industry, reading rooms and computer terminals on worldwide business news and a monograph series on foreign trade.

Florida also has a comprehensive effort to help its firms learn the ins and outs of foreign trade. The Bureau of Trade Development conducts regular export seminars; depending on the level of sophistication of the audience, topics range from a basic "how to" approach to technical discussions of such topics as tariffs, duties, foreign exchange rates, international law, shipping procedures, banking techniques and specific analyses of the export markets in Europe, the Far East and Latin America. In addition to the seminars, the state publishes an *Export Guide,* describing procedures, assistance programs, export service organizations and other export-related information directed specifically for firms with little or no export experience.

A number of states publish inventories of trade leads, frequently compiled with help from the Department of Commerce. Generally computerized, such lists can have maximum impact when cross referenced with lists of in-state firms desiring to export.

A growing number of states are finding conferences and shows a useful device for expanding export markets and cultivating foreign business contacts. In some instances, states work with the federal regional commissions and the Commerce and Agriculture Departments. In addition to making important contacts at these shows, frequently thousands of dollars of goods are bought and sold.

Maintaining computer lists, sponsoring export seminars, publishing trade newsletters and organizing trade shows requires a certain degree of expertise and research capacity for state development agencies. In some cases, states can save money by gathering and expanding upon data collected by other sources—private associations, non-profit business organizations, the federal government. The U.S. Departments of Commerce and Agriculture have extensive research and trade services available, including foreign trade indexes, export mailing lists, trade services, profiles of individual foreign firms, business counseling, foreign market reports and numerous others.

And despite the sometimes fierce competition among states for foreign investment, it is not uncommon to find voluntary associations of states working together to promote foreign trade. One example is the Southeast U.S./Japan Association, an organization of seven states founded to promote friendly relations in trade, culture, industry, technology and commerce.

There is potential abuse in this area, however, when federal funds are involved. A well-designed brochure from the Coastal Plains Regional Commission, colorfully printed in three languages (English, German and French), extols for foreign investors the advantages of the Southeast, including its lower unionization levels and lower hourly wages. A number of state development officials mentioned the many useful services the CPRC provides its five member states. Use of the national taxpayers' dollars to promote a particular region on the basis of its lower wages and union levels raises serious ethical questions, however. Again the thin line between laudable government aid of general economic development and government interference which is prejudicial to one set of taxpayers or regions over another becomes apparent.

APPENDIX A

Table 1
Annual Rate of Employment Change for States
by Growth Rate[1] of State

State Growth Rate	1969-72					
	Births	Deaths	Expansions	Contractions	In	Out
Fast	7.5	5.6	6.2	2.7	.1	.03
Moderate	6.0	5.2	4.7	2.8	.2	.03
Slow	4.5	4.8	4.0	2.9	.03	.03
Decline	3.9	5.1	3.4	3.2	.2	.1
U.S. Average	5.6	5.2	4.7	2.9	.1	.03

	1972-74					
	Births	Deaths	Expansions	Contractions	In	Out
Fast	6.5	4.6	5.8	2.5	.1	.05
Moderate	5.0	4.4	5.0	2.7	.05	.03
Slow	4.3	4.6	4.5	2.9	.2	.1
Decline	—	—	—	—	—	—
U.S. Average	5.5	4.5	5.3	2.6	.1	.05

	1974-76					
	Births	Deaths	Expansions	Contractions	In	Out
Fast	9.5	5.7	5.4	3.1	.2	.05
Moderate	6.9	5.3	4.4	3.3	.1	.1
Slow	6.2	6.1	4.4	3.5	.1	.1
Decline	4.5	5.4	3.6	3.8	.2	.1
U.S. Average	6.7	5.7	4.4	3.4	.1	.1

1. The four classes of employment change are: Fast (over 4 percent per year), Moderate (2 to 4 percent per year), Slow (0 to 2 percent per year) and Decline (less than 0 percent per year). On the average, this break-down divides states into four roughly equal groups, although the size of the groups in any particular year is sensitive to the business cycle.

SOURCE: The Job Generation Process, David L. Birch, MIT Program on Neighborhood and Regional Change, Cambridge, Massachusetts, 1979.

Table 2
**Percent Distribution of New Jobs Created in Each Region
Between 1974 and 1976 by Age of Establishment**

Industry	Region	Age of Establishment				
		0-4	**5-8**	**9-12**	**13+**	**Total**
Manu-facturing	Northeast	67.3%	13.9%	9.3%	9.6%	100%
	North Central	75.4	9.9	8.6	6.1	100
	South	74.1	15.1	6.2	5.9	100
	West	71.0	13.1	8.9	7.0	100
Trade	Northeast	78.2%	9.4%	6.2%	6.1%	100%
	North Central	81.5	8.5	5.4	4.7	100
	South	82.2	8.4	5.1	4.5	100
	West	81.8	8.7	5.1	4.6	100
Service	Northeast	79.4%	8.5%	7.4%	4.7%	100%
	North Central	84.7	7.0	4.6	3.8	100
	South	84.8	7.3	4.3	3.6	100
	West	87.3	5.9	3.4	3.4	100
Total	Northeast	75.5%	10.4%	7.5%	6.6%	100%
	North Central	80.8	8.4	6.0	4.8	100
	South	80.4	9.9	5.1	4.6	100
	West	80.9	8.8	5.5	4.8	100

SOURCE: The Job Generation Process.

Table 3
Percentage of Total Jobs[1] Generated by Size and Status for Regions and the U.S. Between 1960 and 1976

Region	Ownership	0-20	21-50	51-100	101-500	500-1	Total
North	Independent	129.1%	-11.2%	-22.3%	-21.1%	24.3%	98.8%
East	HQ/Branch	36.4	10.5	1.3	-6.6	32.8	8.8
	Parent/Subsidiary	11.6	7.2	3.6	-5.5	-24.4	-7.6
	Totals	177.1	6.5	-17.4	-33.3	-32.9	100.0
North	Independent	52.8%	4.5%	.3%	-2.8%	2.9	57.7
Central	HQ/Branch	12.4	5.8	3.8	4.9	13.1	39.9
	Parent/Subsidiary	2.0	1.7	1.2	1.0	-3.5	2.4
	Totals	67.2	12.0	5.2	3.1	12.4	100.0
South	Independent	42.7%	5.7%	1.5%	0.0%	.4%	50.1%
	HQ/Branch	9.3	4.0	2.9	7.4	16.7	40.3
	Parent/Subsidiary	1.5	1.5	1.1	2.0	3.3	9.6
	Totals	53.5	11.2	5.5	9.4	20.4	100.0
West	Independent	47.8%	5.9%	2.2%	1.9%	2.9%	60.8%
	HQ/Branch	10.0	4.3	3.0	6.2	8.6	32.0
	Parent/Subsidiary	1.7	1.4	1.1	1.8	1.8	7.2
	Totals	59.5	11.6	6.3	9.3	13.3	100.0
U.S.	Independent	51.8%	4.4%	0.0%	-1.5%	3.1%	57.8%
	HQ/Branch	11.9	4.9	3.1	5.6	10.6	36.1
	Parent/Subsidiary	2.3	1.9	1.3	1.1	-.5	6.1
	Totals	66.0	11.2	4.3	5.2	13.3	100.0

1. Total jobs generated in each region are: Northeast (410,890), North Central (1,674,282), South (2,873,619), and West (1,800,112).

SOURCE: *The Job Generation Process.* Page 29: "In this summary table we have netted the major negative components of change (death and contractions) against the positive ones (births and expansions) to obtain a measure of the net contribution to the economy for each region. The figures represent the percentage distribution of total jobs generated in the region. The results tell a clear story. On the average about 60 percent of all jobs in the U.S. are generated by firms with 20 or fewer employees, about 50 percent are created by independent, small entrepreneurs. Large firms (those with over 500 employees) generate less than 15 percent of all net new jobs."

Table 4
Status of Firms vs. Employment Gains by Region,
1969-72, 1972-74, 1974-76

Births
Percent employment gains in firms that are:

	Time Period	Inde-pendent	Head-quarters	Subsidiary	Branch/ HQ in State	Branch/ HQ out of State
Northeast	1969-72	39.0	6.1	5.2	20.3	29.5
	1972-74	35.6	4.1	3.9	21.4	34.9
	1974-76	23.6	2.0	1.4	31.9	41.1
North Central	1969-72	39.7	6.3	3.5	16.0	34.5
	1972-74	30.3	3.5	2.5	20.4	43.3
	1974-76	19.9	1.4	1.1	33.1	44.5
South	1969-72	37.1	5.5	4.6	12.8	39.9
	1972-74	36.2	3.9	3.0	13.9	43.1
	1974-76	25.2	1.6	1.4	21.1	50.6
West	1969-72	40.3	5.5	4.1	20.8	29.4
	1972-74	44.0	4.0	2.5	21.5	28.0
	1974-76	24.0	1.7	1.1	31.6	41.6

Expansions
Percent employment gains in firms that are:

	Time Period	Inde-pendent	Head-quarters	Subsidiary	Branch/ HQ in State	Branch/ HQ out of State
Northeast	1969-72	63.1	16.5	4.2	4.4	11.7
	1972-74	56.2	20.2	5.8	5.7	12.0
	1974-76	58.2	21.1	6.7	4.2	9.8
North Central	1969-72	58.3	15.2	3.0	8.1	15.4
	1972-74	55.4	20.7	4.6	6.0	13.2
	1974-76	54.5	20.9	5.0	6.3	13.3
South	1969-72	59.2	13.3	4.8	4.2	18.5
	1972-74	56.0	15.9	5.0	3.7	19.3
	1974-76	54.2	17.4	5.7	4.6	18.1
West	1969-72	60.4	15.6	3.1	7.5	13.3
	1972-74	58.2	21.0	3.7	6.0	11.0
	1974-76	56.9	22.2	4.6	5.3	11.0

SOURCE: *The Job Generation Process.*

APPENDIX B

Table 5
Regions Ranked by Number of Foreign Projects per Million Persons; Number of Plants, 1975; Number of Acquisitions and Constructions, 1975-1977, Third Quarter; and Number of Constructions, 1975-1977, Third Quarter

	Region	No. of Plants Per Million Persons		Region	No. of Acq. & Const. per Million Persons		Region	No. of Const. per Million Persons
1	New England	15.23	1	Midwest	3.59	1	Southeast	1.60
2	Midwest	13.83	2	New England	2.70	2	New England	1.23
3	Southeast	10.30	3	Southeast	2.33	3	Midwest	1.19
4	Great Lakes	7.97	4	Farwest	1.89	4	Southwest	1.18
5	Rocky Mtns.	7.16	5	Great Lakes	1.76	5	Farwest	.85
6	Southwest	5.45	6	Plains	1.61	6	Great Lakes	.61
7	Plains	5.34	7	Southwest	1.44	7	Plains	.54
8	Farwest	4.74	8	Rocky Mtns.	.86	8	Rocky Mtns.	.17

SOURCE: Based on data from The Conference Board, *Announcements of Foreign Investment in U.S. Manufacturing Industry,* I-1977, III, U.S. Department of Commerce, Bureau of the Census, *Statistical Abstract of the United States 1977.*

Table 6
States Ranked by Number of Foreign Projects per Million Persons; Number of Plants, 1975; Number of Acquisitions and Constructions, 1975-1977, Third Quarter; and Number of Constructions, 1975-1977, Third Quarter

State	No. of Plants Per Million Persons	State	No. of Acq. & Const. per Million Persons	State	No. of Const. per Million Persons
1 New Hampshire	27.23	1 Vermont	10.50	1 South Carolina	4.56
2 South Carolina	25.59	2 Rhode Island	6.47	2 Rhode Island	4.31
3 New Jersey	24.31	3 South Carolina	5.62	3 Vermont	4.20
4 Delaware	24.26	4 Virginia	4.97	4 Virginia	3.97
5 Vermont	21.36	5 New York	4.53	5 Louisiana	2.60
6 Maine	18.11	6 New Jersey	4.36	6 North Carolina	2.38
7 Rhode Island	17.06	7 Louisiana	3.91	7 Connecticut	1.92
8 North Carolina	16.74	8 Delaware	3.44	8 Texas	1.68
9 Connecticut	14.26	9 North Carolina	3.29	9 Delaware	1.72
10 Georgia	13.94	10 Nevada	3.28	10 Nevada	1.64
11 Wyoming	13.81	11 Connecticut	2.89	10 New Jersey	1.64
12 Massachusetts	12.76	12 Pennsylvania	2.44	12 North Dakota	1.56
12 New York	12.26	13 Georgia	2.41	13 Pennsylvania	1.26
14 Kansas	11.92	14 California	2.14	14 New Hampshire	1.22
15 Virginia	11.81	15 Minnesota	2.02	15 Georgia	1.21
16 Idaho	11.31	16 Michigan	1.98	16 New York	1.11
17 Wisconsin	10.73	17 Nebraska	1.93	17 West Virginia	1.10
18 Pennsylvania	10.56	18 Texas	1.92	18 Alabama	1.09
19 Kentucky	10.14	19 Maine	1.87	19 Wisconsin	1.08
20 Maryland	10.03	20 Illinois	1.78	20 California	.93
21 Michigan	9.54	21 Iowa	1.74	21 New Mexico	.86
22 Louisiana	9.30	21 Wisconsin	1.74	22 Illinois	.80
23 Indiana	8.85	23 Massachusetts	1.72	23 Minnesota	.76
24 Illinois	8.24	24 Ohio	1.68	24 Tennessee	.71
25 North Dakota	7.86	25 Missouri	1.67	25 Iowa	.70
26 Mississippi	7.71	26 Alabama	1.64	26 Nebraska	.64
27 West Virginia	7.29	27 North Dakota	1.56	27 Kentucky	.58
28 Texas	6.82	28 Colorado	1.55	28 Ohio	.56
29 Florida	6.79	29 Indiana	1.51	29 Washington	.55
30 Arkansas	6.77	30 Maryland	1.45	30 Maryland	.48
31 Colorado	6.76	31 Oregon	1.29	31 Oregon	.43
32 Missouri	6.29	32 New Hampshire	1.22	32 Mississippi	.42
33 Alabama	5.59	33 Tennessee	1.19	32 Missouri	.42
34 Nebraska	5.19	34 Kentucky	1.17	34 Colorado	.39
35 Utah	5.09	35 West Virginia	1.10	35 Indiana	.38
36 California	4.93	36 Arizona	.88	36 Florida	.36
37 Washington	4.87	37 New Mexico	.86	37 Massachusetts	.34
38 Ohio	4.75	37 Kansas	.86	38 Michigan	.33
39 Tennessee	4.58	39 Mississippi	.85	39 Arizona	.00
40 South Dakota	4.41	40 Utah	.81	39 Arkansas	.00
41 Montana	4.07	41 Florida	.71	39 Idaho	.00
42 Nevada	3.48	42 Washington	.55	39 Kansas	.00
43 Oklahoma	3.36	43 Arkansas	.47	39 Maine	.00
44 Oregon	3.10	44 Idaho	.00	39 Montana	.00
45 Iowa	2.80	44 Montana	.00	39 Oklahoma	.00
46 Arizona	2.78	44 Oklahoma	.00	29 South Dakota	.00
47 Minnesota	2.05	44 South Dakota	.00	39 Utah	.00
48 New Mexico	.89	44 Wyoming	.00	39 Wyoming	.00

SOURCE: Based on data from U.S. Department of Commerce, *Foreign Direct Investment in the United States,* Volume 3, Appendix A, Table 30, pp. A 123-A 125; The Conference Board, *Announcements of Foreign Investment in U.S. Manufacturing Industries,* 1975: I-1977: III; and U.S. Department of Commerce, Bureau of the Census, *Statistical Abstract of the United States 1977.*

The state chart shows some exceptions from regional averages, particularly South Carolina's strong performance.

STUDIES IN STATE DEVELOPMENT POLICY

Please send me the following publications:

Quantity	Title	No.	Price	Total
_____	*State Taxation and Economic Development*	3614	$9.95	_____
_____	*Economic Development:*			
	The Challenge of the 1980s	3610	$9.95	_____
_____	*Innovations in Development Finance*	3612	$9.95	_____
_____	*Labor Market Segmentation*	3611	$8.95	_____
_____	*Inflation and Unemployment*	3618	$8.95	_____
_____	*Democratizing the Development Process*	3616	$7.95	_____
_____	*Job Creation*	3613	$8.95	_____
_____	*Impact Assessment*	3617	$8.95	_____
_____	*The Capital Budget*	3615	$8.95	_____
	TOTAL ORDER			_____

☐ Payment enclosed (no charge for handling and postage)

☐ Please bill me (postage and $2 handling charge will be added)

Payment must accompany all orders under $20.

Name: _____

Title: _____

Address: _____

_____

City, State, Zip _____

Make checks payable to the Council of State Planning Agencies.

Important Note: Discounts of 10% are available on any order of four or more titles. A discount of 20% is available to individuals and institutions ordering the entire nine-volume series ($60.00 per set). Full payment must accompany requests for discounts.